SURVIVAL

SURVIVAL

Tony Boffey

Published in 1991 by
The Self Publishing Association Ltd
Lloyds Bank Chambers,
Upton-upon-Severn,
Worcs.
in conjunction with
Tony Boffey

British Library Cataloguing in Publication Data

A catalogue record for this book is available
from the British Library

ISBN 1 85421 131 5

A MEMBER OF

Designed and Produced by The Self Publishing Association Ltd

Printed and Bound in Great Britain by Hartnolls Ltd, Bodmin, Cornwall

CONTENTS

To Di who typed the original draft

DISCLAIMER

Whilst every care has been taken to ensure the accuracy of this book, no responsibility can be accepted for the results of following all or any of the advice given.

Although most examples have been taken from first or third hand experience all names and references have been changed in order that no individual or company can be identified from the book.

CHAPTER ONE

A Company in trouble – the warning signs

You will find plenty of books and articles offering advice about companies in trouble. Usually these are studies by people who tend to be mathematical, and they concentrate on various financial ratios. If you are a keen commercial accountant, on the other hand, you will have gained a lot from hands on experience, i.e. working in different companies will have given you a 'feel' for when something is wrong. I have known this feeling three times – once in the equivalent of a PLC – and three years later, all three companies had either disappeared or were under new ownership.

So here is my selection of what to look out for.

Points one to eight can all be characterised as a lack of leadership and direction.

1. A lack of tough, genuinely independent non-executive directors, i.e. the board consists of the usual friends; executives of other companies who have some of this company's directors on their board; the titled; the has-beens; the ex-military who still use their rank; the company lawyer and other wallflowers.

2. An unnecessarily grandiose office and reception area for the TYPE and SIZE of business, or expensive premises in an expensive area which the business and the potential from the area cannot justify. Take note – I have known several companies who went bankrupt shortly after installing a fountain in the reception area! Similarly, there is no good reason why companies should insist on

9

having things like office-support services in expensive areas with expensive rents and salaries: £20,000 buys a lot more staff quality in Middlesborough than in Mayfair, or in Warrington rather than in Windsor.

3. Directors who are active in the community, especially those with an active interest in social responsibilities or the arts. They may be using the company's money and resources to support them, with no benefit to the company. This does NOT include those who successfully run a company and in addition are active in these areas. The sort of thing I mean are nationalised industries which second managers to help other companies while parts of their own businesses are in such a mess, they should be holding on to resources, not lending them out.

4. Companies run by ex-politicians who were NOT in business before politics. Those who were in business first can actually be more effective after a political career.

5. Family-based companies two or more generations on from the founder, where the family still dominates the board in numbers and influence, but holds virtually no stock. These will act and think as if the business were still theirs: paying themselves the salaries and perks they believe they need, but could not justify on an open market. I have heard of one finance director whose only apparent qualification was an inability to control his own finances. There is often great scope for turnround or drastic improvement in family companies; and this includes those which have been trading and making profits for years, but have simply never had their potential exploited.

6. The 'number two' man taking over from an autocratic and successful boss. This is even more dangerous if the latter was the founding proprietor and continues to consult for the company. The number two was quite probably a 'yes' man – the only way he would have survived. Either way, he/she will doubtless be unused to leading and being pro-active.

7. Whizz-kids, especially in larger companies where acknowledged high flying, fast track managers come into divisions from group. Their timescale in the job is

at the most a couple of years, after which they will want to be up and off to higher things. The worst will concentrate exclusively on short term results to make themselves look good, emphasising profit against asset building. They lead criticism against the new management who 'fail to perform', and are experts at being promoted up and out before the chickens come home to roost. These are the hardest people to follow into a position – their only interest is in themselves.

8. Companies run by people who look not at the whole business, but only at the function they are used to being involved with and understand (or think they do!) such as:

- a salesman interested only in turnover

- an engineer interested only in technical supremacy

- or a typical ex-auditor accountant interested only in quarterly earnings

Points nine to twenty can all be characterised as poor management.

9. Incorrect Accounting

So-called 'creative accounting' is usually far from creative, and it is usually obvious that this is the case; you might as well put up a sign which says: 'We are trying to fool people'. What a disaster this approach to financial statements is! People who think they are so brilliant they can fool others, are invariably only fooling themselves. Public bodies and government departments are not immune from these practices.

Creative accounting leads to:-

- Capitalisation of research and development expenditure. Remember Rolls Royce 1971?

- Capitalisation of brands – if the brand has value, it should be reflected in an above average return and hence the share price.

- Not covering for doubtful debts as soon as they are known. The actions of many international banks in the last few years have been farcical – if they had been small local companies with such debts, local branches of the same banks would long ago have had them in receivership. Even more amazing, in some cases an international bank will lend more money to a debtor to pay the interest on his overdue loan. Who is trying to fool whom? It is in the directors/ managers' interest to stop criticism, etc. – it is not in the interests of the shareholders.

- Off balance sheet financing. Who is this supposed to fool – some poor, small company creditor? Either the items are required for the business or they are not.

- Quarterly or annual earning myopia. Finance directors may manipulate increases in profits so as to have a steady increase. Those who take in non-existent profits soon get found out if business does not pick up, with terminal consequences for the company. Probably worse are those people who hold back profit in order to have it in hand. If they are conscientious and release it slowly, and profits are genuinely increasing, this will not be too serious for the business. What is really serious is where hidden profits are used to mask present disastrous results. They can show steadily increasing profits only until they run out of their hidden reserves. These are the companies which look successful but get into serious trouble without warning, virtually overnight. Like this:

13

Company X   **(All figures £000's)**

Profits:- made but not shown in accounts,

i.e. in hidden reserve   =   £950

	Yr1	Yr2	Yr3	Yr4
Operating profit	200	400	500	550
Transferred from reserve	400	300	250	NIL
Declared Profit	600	700	750	550
Profits in hand (c/fwd)	550	250	NIL	NIL

- Incorrect treatment of annual payments for services, rental or maintenance to or from the company. This is very common where a percentage of revenue should be taken over the period covered by the service to be provided, but is taken in the period billed.

- (My pet hate) The percentage of completion method of valuing long-term contracts, especially when information on the technical and financial cost to completion is not available or is incomplete.

10. The Annual Report (or the Monthly Management Reports for a Division).

- Is late and becoming later. Perhaps the company management are arguing with auditors about what should go in; perhaps it is trying to prove some significant debts are good; or results are so awful they are being held back as long as possible, in order that the next better report can be released soon after the late bad report or better still, at virtually the same time.

- Published reports are being produced early and getting earlier, month by month or year by year. So quick in fact, that only random testing can be done. I was told of one bank where most results were based on statistical forecasts.

- Annual report is on osententatiously expensive paper; full of pages, but few figures.

- An emphasis on turnover, not profit.

- Going for paper profits and ignoring cash flow.

- Chairman's statement going on about another 'record' year, while results actually show that profits are not even up by the level of inflation; or that the whole gain in profits is due to exchange rate changes, or to acquisitions bought with over-valued paper, thus hiding the operating results of the core business.

- Constantly changing accounting policies, so that comparison of results with the previous years is difficult. (Also watch out for stock rising as a percentage of turnover, especially if it is the work in progress element.)

- A new, expensive corporate logo. This is often seen in companies who have forgotten the Hans Christian Anderson story of the Emperor's New Clothes. The clothes were invisible and so are the unquantified (and therefore unverifiable) benefits to the company.

11. Proliferation of directors' and executives' perks.

Bonuses for performance that start from present salary and profit levels, i.e. they don't have to be earned. Special huge payments for loss of office, often voted through a board meeting as 'ex gratia'.

12. Perks that have no benefit to the company.

For instance, in a public company of unspectacular performance, the managing director drives a Rolls Royce, simply because he wants visible status – but there is no benefit to the company.

13. Nepotism

This is fine if 'number one' son has talent, starts at the bottom and genuinely works his way up. Otherwise, only the non-ambitious, non-family executives remain. These can be of very poor quality, and grossly overpaid for what they are actually contributing to the company.

14. Threat of change

In other words, no concept of product life cycle. This can be fatal in one-product companies (or one-profitable-product companies) which have been milking the same cash cow for a number of years.

15. Sudden death or serious injury to driving force in a one-man led company.

16. Lack of management team

A common problem is where the board consists of members all from the same type of school, university etc., and persists in recruiting similar people to itself, with the same experience and viewpoint on life. This can be great if all is going well, but can be disastrous when markets change, or a wider breadth of vision is required.

17. Risk-taking management

   Chief Executive addicted to gambling with his own money. He is probably gambling with the company rather than taking calculated risks (and if he gambles with the company's money there is very little chance of a turnround).

18. Risk-averse management

   Too much 'playing it safe'. A lot of middle management suffer from this ailment and in many companies it actually gets them promoted: 'Good old Tom has never put a foot wrong' – hardly surprising, he has never done anything. 'George always had his back covered' – that's all he spent his time doing. 'Fred never lost the company any money' – neither did he make it any.

19. Lack of 'no' men

   A need for people who sit back on a regular basis and review the company's markets, products, competition and technological change. These people I would describe as the opposite of company 'yes' men. Let's call them 'third party no men'.

20. Overtrading

   Companies growing fast from overtrading, or having to keep growing fast in order to (a) pay debts, and (b) keep their growth rate up and hence their share price.

21. Finally, let us not forget that a company may also get into trouble for reasons other than poor leadership or poor management. Sometimes it can be the result of pure bad luck and the workings of fate. A firm, for

instance, spends three years carefully building an export market in Kuwait and then, just when it should be reaping the benefit in profits, the country is invaded by Iraq. Similarly, a firm may have found a cheap source of supply from Eastern Europe, only for it to disappear after the 1989 change of regime.

CHAPTER TWO

Cash flow is more important than profit – in the short-term

Concentrating on this principle will at least give you *some freedom of action*. This is probably the most important piece of information in the book.

I am assuming here that a company or division which needs turning around will have high borrowings. This often includes large amounts on overdraft (banks can, and do, call these in at short notice), or short-term loans which banks do not automatically have to renew. A 'facility' at a bank is where you pay a small fee to be able to borrow up to a certain sum of money in a fixed period of time. In addition, you pay interest on the amounts you actually borrow. If you can, get a facility agreed as soon as possible. If your company does have some money, the points which follow are equally valid.

If you concentrate only on book profits the real problems will come to a head later. In any business you need to generate money to pay wages, suppliers, taxes, and often a backlog of debts.

If you can bring in more cash than must go out, you can start to pay your accumulated creditors and then reduce your borrowings. This will save you interest on the loan and then interest on interest and after that, the interest savings snowball.

To achieve this, you must get your staff to think in cash terms.

Ironically, the three groups who naturally think in terms of cash will very rarely have managerial positions. These are:

- Weekly paid workers whose interest is in what their take-home pay is, not the gross

- People used to running a very small business and living from hand to mouth

- People who buy and sell for cash, e.g. market traders.

Middle management, and particularly middle-class ex-students, who are used to a regular salary, a mortgage, annual cost of living increases and the experience of living on overdrafts, are the least cash flow orientated people.

So, withdraw their credit cards and give them a small float. Pay them their expenses by cheque. For those who don't pick up the principle of cash flow quickly, make them wait longer and longer for reimbursement. Once they have had to wait a few times – and been refused reimbursement on some unjustifiable expenses – even the most reticent can turn into cash-hungry executives ON BEHALF OF THE COMPANY. If they don't, and they are not essential, FIRE THEM.

Now, time to work – which is better?

Method A – To sell your product for £10, payments in ninety days?

Method B – To sell your product for £9, payment now?

The product costs £7, paid for thirty days from supply.
Interest paid is at 18% on your borrowings.
The company has an overdraft.
Interest received is 12%

	Month	Month	Month	Month	Month
CASH FLOW	0	1	2	3	4
Method A		-7			+10
Interest paid			-.105	-.106	-.108
Net Cash Flow		-7	-7.105	-7.211	+2.68
Method B	+9	-7			
Interest received		+.09	+.02	+.02	+.02
Net Cash Flow	+9	+2.09	+2.11	+2.13	+2.15

You might say that going for a higher profit and giving credit is better. Well, in this example it is, but who guarantees you are going to get paid at ninety days? (In some countries you can legally enforce a payment date, for example, under the Code of Napoleon.)

No company produces only one unit per month. Let's look at the effect of 1000.

Same product at £7 cost. Of this:-

£5 is materials, bought two months before use on thirty days
£1 is direct labour used when made £0.5 is overhead
£0.5 is sales commission paid when sold, i.e. order taken
1000 sold per month (All figs in £'000's)

METHOD A	1	2	3	4	5	6	7	8	9	10	11	12
Sales		sold			+10	+10	+10	+10	+10	+10	+10	+10
Materials		-5	-5	-5	-5	-5	-5	-5	-5	-5	-5	-5
Labour			-1	-1	-1	-1	-1	-1	-1	-1	-1	-1
Overhead	-.5	-.5	-.5	-.5	-.5	-.5	-.5	-.5	-.5	-.5	-.5	-.5
Commission		-.5	-.5	-.5	-.5	-.5	-.5	-.5	-.5	-.5	-.5	-.5
Operating Cash Flow	-.5	-6	-7	-7	+3	+3	+3	+3	+3	+3	+3	+3
Interest Cost	-.007	-.007	-.097	-.20	-.31	-.27						
Cumulative Flow	-.507	-6.514	-13.61	-20.71	-18.02	-15.29						

You will only have a positive cash flow at the end on the twelfth month. For eleven months you have to finance this business.

Method B. All Figs same as A. Except sales price of £9 paid at time of sale.

METHOD B	1	2	3	4	5	6	7	8	9	10	11	12
Sales		+9	+9	+9	+9	+9	+9	+9	+9	+9	+9	+9
Materials		-5	-5	-5	-5	-5	-5	-5	-5	-5	-5	-5
Labour			-1	-1	-1	-1	-1	-1	-1	-1	-1	-1
Overhead	-.5	-.5	-.5	-.5	-.5	-.5	-.5	-.5	-.5	-.5	-.5	-.5
Commission		-.5	-.5	-.5	-.5	-.5	-.5	-.5	-.5	-.5	-.5	-.5
Operating Cash Flow	-.5	+3	+2	+2	+2	+2	+2	+2	+2	+2	+2	+2
Plus Int Saved	-.007		+.03	+.67	+.107	+.139	+.17	+.20	+.20	+.27	+.3	+.33
Cumulative Flow	-.507	+2.49	+4.52	+7.19	+9.29	+11.42	+13.59	+15.79	+18.02	+20.29	+22.5	+24.92

Method B is positive all year. At the end of the year Method B will have raised £20,000 more cash than Method A. Method A is always at risk from late payment.

At its highest level of net cash outflow, Method A creates negative cash flow of over 20% of the annual turnover on this product.

Your first three months in the company will be absolutely crucial. The first twelve are extremely important.

In addition to the cash flow from individual products, let us look at the cash flow effect of dealing with particular customers.

Product costs £7. In this instance, for simplicity, it is already in stock and we are only going to look at one month's sales.

Delivery cost £5 per £1000. Minimum £5.

COMPANY	A	B	C	D
Size	Large	Medium	Medium	Small
Buys per month	5000	3000	1000	500
Pays	120 days	90 days	60 days	20% deposit - bal 60 days
Delivery	Free to Customer	At Cost	Collects	£7 per 1000
Sales Price	£9	£9	£9.50	£10

CASH FLOW

COMPANY

	A Opera/ting	Cum	Int	B Opera/ting	Cum	Int	C Opera/ting	Cum	Int	D Opera/ting	Cum	Int
MONTH												
0											+1003.5	
1	-35035	-35035	-525	-21015	-21015	315	-7000	-7000	105	-3502.5	-2499	37
2	nil	-35560	-533		-21330	320		-7105	106		-2536	38
											+3.5	
3	nil	-36093	-541		-21650	325	+9500				-4000	
4	nil	-36634	-550	+27015								
5	+45000											
		---			--			--			--	
Interest Cost		2149			960			211			95	

True Profit per Unit

COMPANY	A	B	C	D
Sale Price	+9	+9	+9.5	+10
Cost of Goods	-7	-7	-7	-7
Delivery	-.005	0	nil	+.004
Interest	-.43	-.32	-.21	-.19
	------	---	----	----
Actual Profit	+1.565	1.68	2.29	2.81
Product Cost Sheet Shows	1.995 Profit	2.00	2.5	3.0

(Ignores interest)

In this case the largest customer produces the worst cash flow and profit per unit. This is not unusual. He is big and you need his custom. He also negotiates better. In addition, although taking excessive credit:

(a) He probably pays regularly on the due date, so you can count on his money. You rely on this coming in for the payroll, VAT cheques or whatever large necessary obligations you have.

(b) You can easily factor the debt. This large company is a good credit risk. If the invoice discounters did not want his paper, should you be dealing with him? If they didn't like something about his financial position, can YOU take the risk?

(c) He is taking 50% of your production, and after month five, will start to generate several thousand pounds a month positive cash flow.

NOTE: When this analysis is done, you will find some very unprofitable smaller customers. Apply contribution accounting. Then see if negotiations can improve the position.

So, based on the above analysis, what should your policy be to improve cash flow?

You are making a profit from all four customers (including sufficient to cover financing).

Let us say your overdraft (or better still – 'facility') limit is £125,000. You are currently at £30,000. What if customer A doubled his order? – You would exceed your overdraft limit and risk going into receivership.

Why not see if you could get customer C to buy more or add more customer C-type customers. The maximum effect of such a customer on your overdraft for 5000 units will be:

Units		Cost		Months		
5000	x	7	x	12	=	72,000

Another area to look at is the credit you are getting from suppliers. How important are you to them? They may agree better terms for a short period to help you out.

Cash flow – relationship with confidence

(a) If you ask for a deposit with order, then you may get it. If you DON'T ask, you definitely won't get it.

(b) In the cases where the customer argues about paying a deposit, ask yourself how difficult it will be to collect 100% from him once he has sold on the goods or used the goods and services which you have provided.

A good way to improve cash flow is to eliminate bad debts and unprofitable poor payers.

Help your customers to buy

So they want what you have to offer, at a price you are both happy with. How are they going to pay for these goods and services? The supplier company that helps solve this problem will usually receive the sale. As we will discuss in a later chapter, many small and medium customers judge whether to buy all substantial, and sometimes quite modest, purchases if they can afford the monthly payment. Being able to afford the payment is therefore more crucial to them than the cost of the goods. If they cannot finance the purchase, it does not matter how cheap the item is – they won't be buying it.

So, have a tie with a leasing company, hire purchase company or factor, or other finance source. This will help your business in the following ways:

(a) If your potential customers do not pass their credit checks, should your company, in its more exposed financial position, even consider dealing with them?

(b) If your potential customers pass the finance company's financial check and go ahead with the purchase, your payments are guaranteed from a reliable source, on fixed dates – or better still, up front. The non-bank or non-institution owned factors etc., are often more flexible. They want the business and don't have such a high overhead to carry.

(c) You might get a commission for bringing the deal about, i.e. introducing lender to borrower. If you are not receiving a commission, ask for one!

(d) Like most situations, nothing ensures a better deal for you than healthy competition, so have agreements tied up with at least two companies.

A subsidiary company was judged on profits alone. However, the group chairman would not let the managing director remove any directors or executives. The sales director continued to get the glory from sales to more and more dubious companies with incredible terms of credit. He wasn't bothered: bad debts and interest were costs of the financial function. The results:

Short-term	– profits up, cash flow poor
Medium-term	– profits level, cash flow awful
Long-term	– profits? what profits? – losses, with cash flow so negative it threatened the group's survival.

Our managing director kept trying to collect deposits and put some financial discipline into the company. You can guess who got the blame for the cash position at the end of twelve months. Not the chairman! Not the sales director of the subsidiary – the managing director!. The managing director of the subsidiary had responsibility, but not authority.

Suppliers

If you are short of cash, better credit terms are more important to you than lower costs as long as you are still making a profit. Of course, you will also ask for lower costs on the established principle that if you don't ask you may not receive. You also often find that in the case of a potential turnround situation, suppliers will enforce very tough terms – even for goods and services having only a marginal or no effect on the purchasing company's profitability.

There are three crucial dates for payments for your supplies:

(a) The due date, i.e. the date on which you have agreed to pay or should pay, as per conditions of sale.

(b) A date which is later than (a) but which your supplier has historically accepted. This date changes from supplier to supplier, and even with the same supplier, depending on the economic climate.

(c) A date which is long overdue, virtually non-payment.

Once you get to (c) and cannot improve on your payment position, one or more of the following will happen:

(a) Your suppliers will stop supplying you and demand immediate payment of all monies outstanding to the original due date.

(b) You will have to pay cash for all new supplies, plus a proportion of outstanding debts. In addition, you will usually have to commit yourself to additional payments on other dates and keep them, to clear all outstanding debts. When they say, 'Cash with Order', they will usually mean hard cash, or that they will supply only when your cheque has cleared.

(c) Suppliers will supply at a higher price on a proforma basis and you will have to pay off outstanding amounts and/or give them security. This could be a post-dated cheque/s which will make you personally liable if it bounces in the future. You will usually have little choice if the goods or services are vital to your business.

Cash flow forecast

You need to know the supposed timing of all payments to you, with an estimate of permitted lateness. You also need a list of all payments you should make and when. You will often find that it is a large regularly paid item, such as the payment of VAT every three months, annual company tax etc., which throws your forecasts and plans for cash flow out of line.

You need an estimate for the month of what cash you expect to receive; also, an estimate of the probabilities of your receiving it. This should be done item by item unless there are large numbers of small receipts due. If your incoming cash flow includes large numbers of small payments, somebody will have to estimate what will arrive in total. Use the same person each month, and you can then adjust for their optimism/pessimism.

Keep up to date a list of payments, those which you have

to pay and those which you want to pay, with a reason for each of the latter.

Always treat early or unexpected payments as windfalls. If possible, use them to pay for items which will save you cash in the future. For example, I used to find with contracting companies in the Middle East that, in a period when activity reduced, you could not reduce your labour force as fast as the work was reducing. Employees were entitled both to notice pay and an extra payment based on the number of years worked. All working capital was tied up in work in progress, and there just was not enough cash to pay off that part of the labour force which was idle. It is at those times that a windfall is welcome.

Large customers

Do you allow excessive credit? This is particularly important where you work in a brokerage type business.

> With an airfreight company, 95% of turnover is direct cost. Profit is made on the other 5%, less operating costs. Thus, it is the total finance which you have to watch.
>
> The New York office secured a contract for one division of a major company. Although the office already had a staff of thirty-five, an extra twelve people were recruited and based in another more expensive set of offices, specifically to deal with this one corporate customer who required special paperwork and other extra services. The customer paid ninety days from the end of the month, i.e. in practice one hundred and five days from the date the service was provided!

COMPARISON OF THE TWO OFFICES

	Normal Office 35 Staff	Special Office 12 Staff	
Revenue	1,100,000	1,000,000	Lower Prices
Direct Cost	750,000	750,000	
Gross Profit	350,000	350,000	
Staff	100,000	120,000	Special Tasks /Extra Skill
Office Rent	10,000	20,000	More expensive Location
Other Overheads (Excl.Interest)	60,000	80,000	
NET PROFIT	£ 180,000	£ 30,000	

O.K., the special office wasn't so profitable. 'But', it was said, 'look at the potential. This multi-national has fifteen other divisions and a major international presence.' The element of the calculation forgotten, was that airlines gave the airfreight company only thirty days credit. Most of the special office's direct costs went towards the special services, packing, etc. paid as incurred, i.e. with no credit!

To operate the special office, the following had to be financed monthly :

(a)   Special Services

150,000 of purchase per month and no credit received

$$150,000 \quad x \quad \frac{105}{365} \quad x \quad 12\% \quad = 5178$$

(b)   Airfreight Costs

$$6000,000 \quad x \quad \frac{75}{365} \quad x \quad 12\% \quad = 14794$$

Monthly interest cost 19,972!

This is calculated using only simple interest and not the compound interest which banks and commercial companies use. Thus, the profit of the special division was marginal at best. The customer had negotiated a good deal. Indeed, the multinational used suppliers and potential suppliers to play off against each other, and so obtain very favourable terms.

Three years later, the airfreight company lost the contract. All the special costs, including staff payoffs, had to be made. None of these had been budgeted for. So the work had been done at a loss.

In dealing with creditors, remember that some will continue with legal procedures up to and including a winding up notice, irrespective of the monies they will/will not get as a result, and the cost of doing so.

Company K owed Creditor X £80,000 and had made no payments on old outstanding balances. K promised and promised to pay, its usual policy, when a creditor got upset, being to explain that all the assets of the company were covered by a floating charge in favour of its bank (meaning there were unlikely to be any assets for the unsecured creditors). Thus, if a creditor took legal action, won his case, and put the company into liquidation, he would get nothing. The company would add that it hoped to pay off the debt soon and send a cheque for about 10% – in this instance, about £10,000.

When K put this policy into action, the creditor sent the cheque back. He told K he was going to issue a writ and would wind the company up. K panicked – its directors had personal guarantees which, in the case of a wind-up, would immediately be called in by the bank. K increased its payment to £40,000 – everything it could raise, and the creditor banked it. K promised to clear the balance soon. The creditor just amended the writ and took the company to receivership, from which he eventually received ten pence in the pound, i.e. £4,000 of his now outstanding £40,000. He didn't care: it was his company. The margins were high. All he had lost was his profit on the transaction. If he had not taken the action he probably would have received less money, and who knows when. He was tired of being treated with contempt.

Look therefore for all possible ways to improve the timing of overall cash flows *without destroying the company's future*. By getting as many people in the company as possible, to think and act in terms of cash flow, you will probably have done more to ensure the company's survival than by any other of your actions.

Explain to the staff that a positive cash flow protects their COMPANY, their JOBS, and their FUTURE.

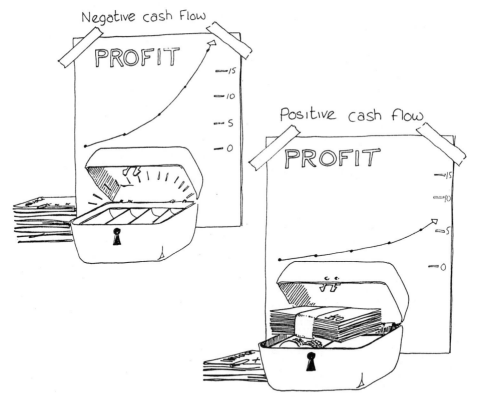

You cannot spend book profits!

33

CHAPTER THREE

The First Day

Remember not all companies can be turned round.
Speed is essential – as is a good sense of humour.

You have been asked to turn a company around and you may be going in from any one of a number of angles – sent in by group, owners or bank. Each company in trouble is different but certain actions will be required.

Much depends on how much reading you have done in advance; what information you have gained; what knowledge you have of the company, its industry, key staff etc; whether you have had access to the accounts, particularly monthly management accounts, organisation charts and sales figures; and how well you really know the industry, the type of business and its products.

This is my general list of actions. Take what is of use to you. Do not treat it as a Bible.

ACT 1 – Take authority over all company payments.

> Much of this may be delegated quite quickly, but control by you is essential.

ACT 2 – Take control of purchasing.

> Until you approve it, nothing is to be purchased.
> Again there will be a great deal of delegation, very
> quickly. First to be delegated will be items in agreed
> budgets which are on target, and I mean budgets
> agreed by you. In many badly run companies, a cost
> budget is simply based on last year's actual cost (i.e.
> what was spent) plus a percentage. This invariably
> leads to over-spending.

ACT 3 – Find the company, office, factory grapevine(s).

> Tea ladies, cleaners, receptionists, typing pools, mail
> rooms, company drivers, odd job and security men,
> are all excellent places to start. Other useful sources
> of information are employees close to retirement,
> or those working a few hours a week after
> retirement.

ACT 4 – Take control of all promotions, transfers and
changes in staff.

> Make sure this includes agency staff – and don't
> forget staff benefits.

In one firm the manager was steadily given more authority by
the partner. He kept adding benefits; his accountant also
benefited. Their creative accounting cost a fortune when the
market turned down, i.e. they had capitalised every possible
expense. They never considered any debt no matter how old
dubious or bad. Their cost cut off was awful. Not surprising
really, the manager was paid a percentage of profits and the less
costs booked, the better for him – not the company!

ACT 5 – Hold an office meeting with supervisors – directors
not present.

Also, hold one at your manufacturing sites – depending, of course, on how many you have. Try to find out who is *actually* running the company, not who is *supposed* to be. Often, the people actually making things happen will have been working very hard, under enormous pressure and with only implied authority.

ACT 6 – Find a good secretary/personal administrator.

Either take a secretary with you, pick up somebody pre-selected, or if you are not impressed with what is available, get somebody from an agency. This person is to be your number one assistant, indeed, an extension of yourself.

ACT 7 – Spend an hour with the Sales Director.

Just listen and ask questions. After that, meet individually the two worst and two best performing salesmen, as well as one who has been there six months and one a year. Listen and prompt comment. Then listen to them together. Next, arrange to meet the most important customers as soon as possible. You will probably need to visit with one of your people who normally makes contact with the customer.

ACT 8 – Spend an hour with the Production Director.

Do the same with each department head, and with the foreman. If you have a company factory union, arrange a meeting with a local official, followed by a meeting with the company representatives.

ACT 9 – Where possible, eat in staff or works canteen.

Perhaps have a table allocated. The staff will then see you are human and are with them, not off in some ivory tower.

ACT 10 – Approve all senior managers' expenses, budgets and actual expenditure.

This will give you control of them where they will appreciate it, i.e. in the pocket.

ACT 11 – Find out the present and projected cash flow.

Look at any budgets produced in the last 6 months and compare them with actual expenditure. Have a list prepared of who will be out and where in the next three weeks, and make sure it is up-dated daily. This should cover all senior executives and sales representatives and anybody else you want to keep track of.

Is there product costing? Review it. Obviously if you have 7000 products you will need to look first at the main sales lines and assumptions used in the costing. A key piece of information is competitors' prices. Find the position on 'aged' debtors and creditors. Check stock levels by category and list what has not moved for six months. If the information is not avialable, get it prepared immediately.

Remember, you need information. It doesn't need typing out. You want what information is available, when it is available; and you need it in a form you can digest, i.e. three figures on the back of an envelope is often more useful than a thirty page report. If it comes bound in a nice folder, rip it up and throw it in the bin. Get the message over that information is to be used, not worshipped.

ACT 12 – Check the payroll.

If it is too high, people are going to have to be removed. Identify somebody (the more senior the better) to fire, and do it on your first day. The message is then clear – things are going to change. Anybody can be affected. This new man/woman means business.

ACT 13 – Have the customer complaints file for the last six months brought in.

What – no complaints? So why are you in trouble?

ACT 14 – Review major advertising or promotional campaigns.

This includes those in progress, as well as commitments due. Do this as fast as possible. You may not have this money to spend again, soon – or ever.

ACT 15 – Go somewhere where you can see the competitors' products/sales offices.

Or make arrangements to do this in your first ten days.

ACT 16 – Walk around your facilities.

Obtain plans of layout. WALK, LOOK AND TALK. THEN DO IT AGAIN. Over the next few weeks, repeat this procedure. Obviously much depends on the size of the company and the number of locations; for example, if you have six factories and twenty-seven offices, then to visit all of them initially would take all your time, the commodity you have the least of. However, do it with at least two and get hold of plans and photographs of others; also, videos if necessary. Arrange to be at a factory when the men come into work one day, and ditto the night shift. Go into the design laboratory at weekends or the accounts office in the evening.

ACT 17 – Phone up all company locations as a potential customer.

See what happens! By all, I mean ALL.

ACT 18 – Review inbound and outbound communication.

Do this as much as possible, on a regular basis. Remember, you are looking for information, not acting as a reviewer of grammar.

ACT 19 – Arrange to give an interview to the local paper within ten days.

Especially if your main factory is in one area. Make sure that you are given a tough interview by your own people first.

ACT 20 – Spend half an hour at the bank.

>Unless, of course, you have been put into the company by the bank. Do this by Day Three at the latest. Also arrange other half hour visits in the first week with two other banks.

ACT 21 – Refuse to sign all contracts until you have reviewed them.

>If any large projects are in progress, exactly where is the company with them? Don't believe your in-house technical estimates until you have had them checked. Review any large capital works in progress. You are doing this not to see it if will make a profit but whether it is within budget. All projects start off within budget, you need to see they stay there.

ACT 22 – Find out if there are any legal cases in progress.

>Whether for or against the Company. Ask the Company's solicitors the time scale, likely costs, chances of winning. Are there any cases about to come up? Who would know?

ACT 23 – Have organisation charts drawn up for all departments.

>These should include details of age, years in job, years with company. Try to put a face to staff names, and then first names to surnames. If necessary have somebody Polaroid the company. Note: I said company.

ACT 24 – Arrange a precis on directors and senior employees.

>Check personnel files. Then you want to know the outline of salary packages, plus salary bands for the

whole company. Review all employees earning 20% more than basic in last month and year to date. Why? Some of these people may be the answer to your problems, others at least part of the problem.

ACT 25 – TAKE CONTROL – LEAD FROM THE FRONT.

Make as many decisions on the first day that you can make. It will be a sign of change.

ACT 26 – The first mistake you make, talk about it.

This sometimes makes other people open up. You have a lot to learn – quickly.

ACT 27 – If possible, arrange a second office that only your secretary knows about.

You should spend two hours a day in here thinking and planning. When you come out, return calls and get things done.

ACT 28 – Get a daily list of money received wherever you are – also check on 'aged' debtors and creditors.

ACT 29 – At the end of the day write down:

- What are the most important things I need to know?
- What are the most important things I have done?
- What do I intend to achieve tomorrow?
- Which task do I least want to do? Put this one at the top of your list if you are avoiding it, it almost certainly needs doing.

Now get a good night's sleep, you're going to have plenty to do.

'Oh', you say, 'nobody can get all this organised on Day One.'

If you want to meet somebody who has done it, my name is on the cover of the book!

CHAPTER FOUR

Terms of trading and collecting debts

Terms of trade

Does the company actually have terms of trading?

This is the small print you find on the back of orders, quotations, order acknowledgements, etc. Has anybody ever reviewed it? When? Who?

Do your people understand basic contract law, particularly offer and acceptance?

In many cases they don't. Even companies with seemingly foolproof terms of trade often find that, because they accepted another document from their potential customer, the customer's terms of trade are those that govern the contract. I suggest you let your commercial solicitor loose for a fixed fee so he can recommend:

- What he thinks is wrong – in layman's terms.
- What could potentially happen – a practical not theoretical exercise.
- The cost to have it corrected and how long will this will take.

Don't forget to consult your printer as well. Once the terms of trade have been revised, get your stationery reprinted with them; if you already have a stock of stationery just attach your terms with a staple. It is particularly important to state the country of jurisdiction for the transaction. Scotland has different law to England, for instance, and in the U.S.A. state laws' differ, i.e. what works in Alabama is ineffective in Oregon.

Any legal cases you have in the future, for collection of debts for goods and services provided, will depend on these terms of trading and the actions of your staff. It would be a good idea to have two half-day sessions on contract law: one for people buying and one for people selling.The amount of ignorance is surprising. Often, the only person in a company with any knowledge of the subject – the accountant – is neither engaged in, nor controls any sales activity, and even his knowledge may be incomplete or out of date.

Collection of debts

What has not been billed?

In most companies in a turnround situation, this will be a worse problem than that of the outstanding creditors. This is because it is hidden. Your problem is not only what debts have not been collected, but what goods or services you provided that have not been invoiced.

'What utter rubbish,' you may say. 'Big companies have controls which ensure that this does not happen.' Not true, such controls are expensive to install and need to be continually monitored. Many small and medium-sized companies either don't have them, or don't observe them. For instance:

- If nobody raises a despatch note, no invoice will be raised.

- If visit sheets are not completed, nobody bills for the repair call.

- If extra costs are incurred on a contract but nobody is checking if reimbursable, they will not get billed.

- If somebody asks for extra work on a construction site

or modification in a factory, and it is not recorded, it will not be billed. Also, if it is requested in writing, the client representative may not have the authority to authorise the modifications.

- Nobody may raise an invoice for the last work done on a contract. Once it has been forgotten for six months, the chances of it being found are small. (Forget the auditors, they need a trail to follow). I saw this happen myself, in the period 1987 – 1990. So, personally ensure that everything is billed, or you will never collect the money.

Has the right quantity been billed?

This is a very common error. Deliver two – invoice for one. How can this happen? – The contract is for supply, the customer decides to have an extra unit which he requests whilst it is being installed. Very often the extra unit is missed.

Has the right quality been billed?

One is charged at £200 per ton and one at £800; the people in accounts are not technical; the paperwork is untidy and off goes the invoice at £200. It may be found from the stock records – although in many small companies, these are in such a mess it is only when an annual count takes place that stock records are amended to actuals, and even then there is often not the time to investigate discrepancies. Not charging for the annual rental or maintenance is common. So is forgetting to increase the prices.

Is it at the right price?

It is amazing how often companies go on issuing invoices at

old prices, and nobody picks this up. Also common is where several customers have negotiated different prices for the same item.

Are customers entitled to a discount?

How many customers are given a quantity discount for one item or a one-off special occasion and from then on always put it on their purchase orders? The company raises invoices from this. Equally common are the companies which deduct an early payment discount when they pay well past the due date. Ask for it back! Not charging for delivery is also common.

NOTE: All of the above may be classed as inefficiency – not fraud, though this also occurs, as illustrated below.

> The company was an importer of a quality food product. The police paid a visit to check up on cans of the company product which were being sold very cheaply (20% of retail) at a local market. The company had no recorded stock shortages and were puzzled. Initial investigations concentrated on possible misuse of labels. What had actually happened was that nobody was counting the cases going out on pallets. They went past a mechanical counter. Certain items were taken off and sent past again. The extras were sent out with a colluding driver. The culprits had been stealing one hundred cases a week for some time. Customers were only reporting about fifty per week as not arriving.

Are the dates correct?

Most people use some type of mechanised 'aged debtors' (hopefully with an open items list). So, let's say you decide as a policy to chase all debts over sixty days; watch out for the following:

(a) Work incomplete, not done, or invoiced early to get the figures in.

(b) Contract not specifying what will be paid and when. Until the work is certified by an independent third party, you are not entitled to payment, no matter how old your invoices are.

(c) Work completed, or goods supplied, several months ago. It was discovered, that it had not been invoiced when supplied and invoiced it on the date found. So the true age of the sixty day debt is now one hundred and twenty days, two hundred and ten days etc.

(d) Because the aged debt was causing problems for the directors of a subsidiary or the manager of an operating department, a credit note was raised and the work re-invoiced.

(e) In the case of a foreign sale, the company has used:

- date left factory

- date left country

- date arrived country

- date arrived customer

– none of which is very meaningful if it is being settled by letter of credit, which specifies exactly how many days after a specified event you should be paid.

(f) Work still not started or not finished. Perhaps invoiced early at client's request due to budget reasons, i.e. some public body with money left over in its budget, desperate to spend it before losing it.

Is the debt due?

Are there any special terms in operation which mean the money is not outstanding now?

Are there disputed items, for example:

- quantity
- price
- quality of work done
- damage or breakages
- late delivery
- non completion

Now we are ready to start collecting debts

1. Stop sending statements. Only send them to customers who pay on them.

2. Find out the true composition of the debt, i.e. what is actually believed to be owed. Get details of all invoices and any unallocated cash.

Collecting a debt from Mr Smith

Mr Smith has recently moved from Glasgow to Brighton. His company is based for accounting purposes in London. The move was therefore organised either by the personnel officer in Glasgow, a Mr Brown; or by the personnel officer in Brighton, Mr White; or by the personnel officer in London, Mr Black.

A search is therefore needed under all the above names in each ledger to try to match cash with an invoice before you can see what to collect. The situation is only going to get worse; so, before continuing with collecting money, stop the sales ledger posting any cash until it identifies which account and invoices it was paying.

3. Which customers have a history of being bad payers?

4. With whom do you hope to do significant business in the future? Remember: a customer is a person who pays his bills.

A customer pays for his goods   *Potential customer*

5. See what correspondence is available in the organisation. It could be in medium-sized firms in any of several departments. Have it sorted into alphabetical order.

6. Pick out some large old accounts with relatively few transactions. Get hold of somebody at the other company. You can be referred from site to site, and then person to person. Keep recording names of who referred you to whom and telephone/fax numbers and talk to each person. If you cannot get them, telex them, fax

them, send recorded delivery letters. If their office/ factory is not too far away, or if the debt is a large one, turn up in person.

7.   Once you are convinced the debt is genuine and the debtor just won't pay, let a commercial solicitor loose. Instruct him whether you want to keep the account, i.e. do future business, then agree action. Most solicitor seven-day letters are a waste of time. If you need cash, keep going right through the system as fast as possible to a winding up notice. If it is possible to prove an individual rather than the company itself is potentially liable, you could get your cash much faster.

A major problem arises when you have started action, and then people in your company get involved in discussions and even correspondence with people in the debtor company. This automatically affects and back- dates your legal action. If a company has a poor collection record, you will often find that its own management and staff have reasons for not being paid now for work.

8.   Clear up small debts. Having tried one solicitors letter, let the debt collectors loose. It never ceases to amaze me what they can bring in. Debt collectors work for a percentage of collections. This is often very high. However, better 85% now, than 100% eighteen months from now, when your company has been in liquidation for a year.

9.   Have a credit check on large debtors. Seek a significant payment, followed by regular reduction of debt. When they miss what they have promised, for whatever reason, and you cannot get in touch immediately with your contact, put the debt out to a solicitor.

10. Apply constant steady action to reduce aged debts. Don't ignore the recent debts by concentrating just on the old ones.

The best person I ever saw for collecting money was a lady who automatically phoned up every account once it reached forty-five days. She talked to the debtors as if she had known them for years and they could not do enough for her. Money constantly came in on time. Equally, companies continued to do business with her.

You have to take each company as it comes. I try to use and train my clients' staff to do as much of the work as possible. It can be very unpleasant work. People will be rude to you; they may shout and swear. They will go over your head to the managing director, the group chairman, or even well connected non-executive directors – this shows you are having an effect. Sometimes you are applying pressure on companies in a very precarious position. If you don't, somebody else will. They will be paid and you will be left with the unsecured creditors on the statement of affairs, lucky to get ten pence in the pound two years later.

CHAPTER FIVE

Purchasing – Get it Under Control

Sounds obvious, but in many troubled organisations, everybody and his dog will be purchasing. There will be little formal paperwork; invoices will be paid more than once (I've even heard of divisions of national companies which regularly pay credit notes!); credit will neither be negotiated nor taken; and companies will pay for damaged goods, or goods and services not received. Where systems do not exist or are incomplete, chaos reigns. You are reliant on people. It doesn't matter how good your system is if the people operating it have not been trained to use it properly.

- I was in Iran in 1976. The newly-arrived building foreman needed a mobile tower crane. So he went down to the supply yard, told the man in charge and stated that it was urgent. All three cranes were out on jobs, so the stores supervisor bought another one for £20,000+. This was for a three day job!

- Central buying had control. Nothing without a purchase order would be paid for and the suppliers had been informed. So, the senior engineer purchased whatever he needed on his company credit card.

Another problem with a company in trouble is the ability of staff and directors to waste money on non-essentials.

In Riyadh we were always desperately short of money, but the managing director decided we needed a proper meeting room and, despite protests, spent £5000 on having it decorated! It was a small company and had been on the brink of bankruptcy for virtually all of its independent existence. Money was owed over credit terms to all suppliers.

In a U.K. company, when the cash situation was awful, the management made and enforced the following purchasing decisions:

(a) To renovate the top floor of their offices and to carpet the whole office – totalling about £2000 of expenditure. Business could have continued without this for at least another twelve months. The expenditure had no positive effect on profits, and a negative effect on cash control.

(b) To have a corporate video. For the type of product this was the perfect medium. A bargain price was obtained and sales would start to come in as a direct result nine months after it was finished, but only slowly at first. Again, it nearly took the company under. In addition to the effect on cash flow, much management time was taken from sales and debt collecting, and this helped to worsen the already bad cash position. As the company did survive, in retrospect it was a good purchasing decision, but it could have been fatal.

Sometimes inefficient purchasing can lead to greater profits!

The Java Sea Restaurant

We were paid so much a day for our drilling contract. Our food cost was twice budget. The accountant went out to a rig. He found more than three months stock of many items and that we were virtually running a five star restaurant. The accountant's work with our Swiss chef brought the food cost down from $20 to $10 per man per day. Independently the deputy regional manager went round to the oil company and and had the fee increased to cover $20 per day. Result – more profit all round.

Budget	Original Cost	Renegotiated Fee	Reorganized Cost
$15 per man	$20 per man	$20 per man	$10 per man

So with 60 men we were making $18,000 more per month

On a reimbursable expense, we were now making a profit!

So what do we need to do?

1. Priority in purchasing must be for goods and services which have a direct positive effect on cash flow and profits.

    In addition, items of safety equipment required by law or because you need them should also go ahead. Why? Because your workforce is probably demoralised. They have been expecting the place to close. They probably still do. Your controls are starting to bite. There is little prospect of any extra take-home pay in the near future. So when they see the small amount of money being spent on their safety, they appreciate it.

2. Priorities must be linked to production and sales.

    One possible reasons for a company's being in trouble, is overstocking. So, although you may have given an item priority, this does not mean the purchasers should just keep buying what quantities they feel like. Do you know

54

lead times? What are your present stocks? Production schedules? Sales forecasts?

Also, don't forget sales (not marketing) is vital in the short term. Don't cut the advertising unless you know it is a waste of money. If you do know that, how are you going to re-deploy those funds? Similarly, if a salesman is hitting target and is due for, and expects a new vehicle, he should get it and not have to wait six months simply because of a rigid new purchasing policy.

3. Introduce purchase orders throughout the organisation – fast,

    To be applied with common sense! Inform all suppliers in writing by recorded delivery or the equivalent, that only orders written out on official purchase order forms will be accepted. Initially in many cases their sales people will continue to supply. When payments are stopped for not being covered by an official order, the message will get home.

4. Controlling Overheads.

    You cannot beat budgetary control. Let a department have a budget. It can switch between expenditure categories, but should be controlled on total. Don't just leave departments to it; for example, with Advertising you need to see the plan for the year, otherwise it may spend its allocation in three months and have none left for the peak seasons.

5. How professional is purchasing?

    Exactly what is the background of your purchasing staff? Have they worked in other functions, other companies? What do they see their role to be? How do they measure their contribution to the company, their efficiency ?

Is there a prima donna in charge, or perhaps a little Hitler?

Some of the worst purchasers are ex-reps. They can make life very unpleasant, especially for the small supplier salesperson. These small company owners are the people who can often give you flexibility and service.

Do you have more than one source of supply for key items? Is anybody developing new suppliers to give you flexibility? Are you placing any orders with these people?

6.   Who makes the purchasing decision?

Which supplier/s do you use. Is the company always buying from one supplier? Favouritism and corruption can be rampant:

*   Fred went to my school/university

*   He went to the right type of school

- He is from my part of the country

- He is a relative

- He is also Jewish/Protestant/Catholic/Muslim, a member of my Golf Club, Tiddlywinks society, or whatever. If not maybe his wife, daughter, or sister is.

I always buy my computer stationary from my friend Fred.

In Riyadh, one English technician was so mean and unhelpful he would borrow money from his labourers to buy food if the daily allowance was a day late. He was always moaning. However, he was 'helpful' in going to buy electrical supplies. He would even go in his own time. Yes, he was pocketing the 15-20% cash rebate.

7. Do they take quality into account?

Some purchasers only concentrate on price. Is there feedback from the company on the quality of goods and services received?

A firm had a fleet of lorries and bought a bargain load of tyres at only 10% of normal price. The quality was awful and rather than thirty thousand miles per tyre they got only one thousand miles or less. Plus all the extra costs of breakdowns.

8. Getting the best price.

Do the purchasing staff know the tolerances? Do they take into account credit period? There are suppliers who will put stock on your site, or keep it on theirs for you to call off. You are only invoiced when you use it. Thus you have back-up supplies at no extra cost. Maybe the items are more expensive, but overall, from a cash flow point of view, it is cheaper and more beneficial .

Are there other costs involved rather than product prices? How do delivery, packaging, insurance compare?

9. Quotes for a period.

Do you know how long the supplier will hold this price, or will you find that the lowest quote supplier is the most expensive when the invoice comes in?

Do you put prices on the purchase order? It's amazing how often firms don't. Prices may be higher than now. O.K., so you give an open cheque. Put on: 'not more than X pounds'.

10. Signing purchase orders.

Initially take over yourself. Then delegate fast.

So, you think that's purchasing under control? No, that's just the obvious purchasing. What is the biggest controllable cost that is not controlled in most companies? – THE TELEPHONE.

No, I don't mean stop all calls or the office junior making a dental appointment.

There are two chief aspects where telephone use can be controlled:

(a) Waste.

Usually senior and middle managers. They never plan a call. Nor do they plan when they make it, nor do they make notes of the call. So was it important ?

Does everybody need a phone with a direct dialling facility? Is it too easy for your staff to call Australia or wherever? (Remember, it is certainly cheaper than going there or phoning from home.) Is there anyone to train the staff in how to make a call, or the differential costs of calling at different times?

(b) Unauthorised use.

In one office where I worked, the only phone that could be used internationally had a lock on it.

Other wastage

The Direct Debit

It is amazing what you will find you are subscribing to, and once signed, they run for ever.

Expense Claims

All sorts of garbage will find its way into this category: books people have decided to buy, meals for visiting staff etc. Again, apply common sense. If somebody who left home at six a.m. and installed two computer systems, spent £30 on an evening meal, so what? This is far more justified than the £5 a manager spent on refreshments whilst visiting an exhibition with no possibility of extra profit to the company.

Similarly, supposing a workman is out on a job and does not have the £2 worth of parts in his kit required for the repair. So he buys them from a local shop. Congratulate him, he could have come all the way back, wasting his time and fuel.

Expenses should be controlled with a view to their potential advantage to the company, not by rules about being fair or who at what grade is entitled to what. My preferred method is to control by profit centre. This removes the need for petty rules, and hours spent checking. Incidentally, most people are not alert to receiving VAT receipts. In the U.K. this alone can save nearly 15% off expenditure.

Other expenses

(a) Accommodation Costs

Some people just like spending money. Particularly other people's. It has been my experience that entertainment costs usually rise the further you get away from an action creating profits. Middle management of staff departments especially need watching. Do you get the benefit of corporate rates – if not why not? Many people who travel often just want a reasonable standard of room without a lot of fuss. Ditto with meals.

(b) Credit Cards

With these you are controlling after the event, i.e. you are not controlling. Your bank account will be hit by the expenditure. If people cannot behave, withdraw their corporate cards, or enforce limits on them. In my opinion, credit cards are far more efficient than large cash floats. Try to get staff to use their own.

(c) Fuel (use of vehicles)

Also, maintenance costs (which probably amount to more than fuel). A lot of people still believe that travel is action. Have you noticed how many business trips to scenic areas take place at the time of year when the weather is best? I would suggest you have no hard and fast rules; it is your company – you run it.

BUT

- It can be more cost-effective to fly from London to Manchester – no overnight stop and no hours wasted on motorway

- An overnight train sleeper could be more effective

- It is not the relative or even the absolute cost of travel that is crucial. If you are sending somebody to Japan, presumably you want them to be fresh and alert when he starts working. If there are thousands, or tens of thousands of pounds involved, companies should be more willing to incur higher costs. Who can say they are wrong or right? You can only measure by the results.

(d) Misuse of vehicles

Very common – or is it?

- Visiting Hong Kong I arranged with the hotel for a taxi to the airport. A huge Mercedes limousine turned up. You could have put twenty people in it (same cost as normal fare) – obviously somebody was moonlighting with the employer's vehicle.

- In the U.K. for some crazy reason, all employees with company cars received free petrol. Most people did not abuse this. However, one engineer managed to spend the equivalent of two thousand miles worth of private petrol every week. Another employee who did not go out on business was spending (well, the company was) the equivalent of over one thousand miles a week of private petrol. In both cases, receipts came in from everywhere.

- Sometimes the employee does the company a favour. A firm's premises were insecure, so an employee was asked to take a pool vehicle home for the weekend for safety.

In general, getting expenditure under control depends on the size, type and cost structure of your company. In a production orientated company of two hundred people with seven office staff and three company vehicles, no matter how much effort you put into controlling telephone and car costs, you won't save much. It would be better having some other costs analysed, for example, material handling, consumable tools etc.

(e) Borrowing of equipment

Either with or without permission: tools, typewriters, computers etc.

(f) Space

You can only save money if you can sublet the spare space you have created or can release other rented space by bringing people back into your main buildings. You will find enormous resistance. Look at all the potentially prime site buildings the U.K. Civil Service manages to retain in Central London. Why are the administration departments of most charities based in London?

Space does not just mean office space. You can sublet factory and warehouse space, and in some countries, retail space. Even spare tarmac can be sub-let for parking.

(g) Stationery

I suspect that in a large, computer-age office, more money could be saved on stationery, especially computer stationery, than on any other, excluding salaries. One of my definitions of a well-run office from a cost point of view is where old forms, or the backs of non-confidential computer printouts are used, instead of the traditional A4 scrap pads.

- My visit to an Irish animal foods company was coming to an end. On the last day I had some spare time. O.K., a chance to look into stationery. I discovered that for 8 office staff there were over seventy varieties of envelopes! Old supplies were never used up. Round would come the rep. and the office manageress would buy for the year based on last year's cost, plus a bit. She never looked at what they still had in stock.

- There were two thousand factory workers on a site of about fifty departments. Looking at consumable tools, I took a quick flick through the stores issue dockets (a great technique but never in any management books!) and noticed that rather a lot of screwdrivers were being issued. So I had an analysis done, which took a day to complete. Over 50% of issues were going to one department of only twenty men. Indeed, this department was being issued with one hundred and fifty per week. One of the employee's brothers had a market stall!

Remember, when it comes to expense accounts, your staff need to know that most things are negotiable. If they don't ask they don't get. You can only say no.

Conclusion

Get your purchasing under control – FAST.

NO cost is too small or too vital not to be questioned. It takes longer to get some costs under control due to contracts already signed.

Start justifying every purchase (cost). The fancy name for it is Zero Based Budgeting – and it WORKS.

CHAPTER SIX

Creditors – be truthful

In the previous chapter you were doing your best to get purchasing under control. Now you have to deal with a mass of OVERDUE debts. Many of the people you are dealing with are fed up. They will no longer supply you. If they do, it is only by cash with order, plus a proportion of the outstanding debt.

The company has made promises for months and broken virtually every one. It has ignored credit terms, paid something on account and panicked when the red final demands started to come in.

The principal of one company told me: 'My last accountant spent all his time on the phone, he did nothing else. Once they got hold of him he paid everything, no order or priority, ran the overdraft up over the limit.'

Indeed, he had an average of £200,000 overdrawn against a limit of £160,000. Looking further back I found that before his appointment, £240,000 had often been reached. So the problem was not new, neither was the previous accountant at fault.

You get recruits from large companies used to paying all of a monthly amount by statement. This can be disastrous in small companies in the turnround situation. You are also paying the salaries at the month end. The account then gets hit with the interest.

Regular payment, little and often, will keep more people happier. Although it will thrill none of them, it will take some pressure off you.

Trying to dodge creditors gets you this kind of response:

'I would like to speak to your Mrs X who has recently had such an active personal life as to leave me breathless. To my personal knowledge she has, in less than four weeks, attended the funerals of three close relatives; been to the weddings of three of her sons and her mother; taken six days annual holiday at no notice and for one day at a time; been to the dentist three times, the doctors twice and the hospital on another occasion; AND been in urgent, continuous meetings for the rest of the time.'

Nothing is more frustrating than phoning up and getting the standard 'brush off'. It will drive your switchboard crazy because they are the ones getting all the abuse.

If you take all phone calls when you receive them, you will do nothing else. In the meantime, you will have to deal with sacks of post, statements and demands. It is, however, vital that you talk to people. I used to sit down in one company at four p.m. each day and deal with all inbound calls of the previous twenty-four hours, i.e. phoning them back.

Never promise people you will pay them when you have no intention of doing so. A good deal of trust will be lost and you will have to spend time building it up again. In the past, if I have promised to pay something by a certain date, I do. It is rarely all that is due, but I keep my word. My experience is that little and often is better than feast and famine, especially if your company has a history of poor payments and broken promises.

Company Y owed £20,000 – on stop, very little paid, usually something every three months.

	FEAST AND FAMINE		LITTLE AND OFTEN	
	Pay	Outstanding Balance	Pay	Outstanding Balance
Week 1		20,000	1000	19,000
Week 2		20,000	250	18,750
Week 3		20,000	250	18,500
Week 4	2000	18,000	250	18,250
Week 5		18,000	250	18,000
Week 6		18,000	500	17,500
Week 7		18,000	500	17,000
Week 8	2000	16,000	1000	16,000
Week 9		16,000	500	15,500
Week 10	2000	14,000	500	15,000

You will have less problem with the second procedure. You are consistently reducing the debt.

Before you start taking control of the payments, ensure you know what a shadow director is. Also, find out from your commercial solicitor or auditor what insolvency is. In both cases you could have significant personal liability. Make sure you have figures to monitor it. This is even more important if you are a consultant or a third party.

Some people you HAVE to pay; for instance:

(a) The telephone, electricity and gas companies who will cut you off.

(b) In the U.K. if you are using gas in engineering you will have to pay British Oxygen, or no supply.

(c) Interest and charges which will automatically hit the bank account along with any standing orders and direct debits. Company credit cards are another nightmare.

(d) Income Tax deductions and Value Added Tax. If you cannot pay all, pay some and state the reason why you have not paid the rest. If you are truthful, they can be very helpful.

> A client was due to pay around £35,000 in VAT. A major contractor owed him £25,000 and all of it was VAT which we had tried to collect for weeks before. So, we went and told our VAT office the problem, and showed them correspondence and the legal action which we were taking. When the time to pay came, we paid £10,000. We then paid the balance four weeks later when legal action had been successful, with no VAT penalty.

Under the new rules, it may well be that you incur penalties, but if you don't, always explain your problem: your eventual situation could be much worse.

Other things being equal, you have to pay companies from whom you are getting those supplies and services which keep the money-producing parts of the business going. However, people with whom you are no longer in a commercial relationship with, are more likely to take legal action, up to and including a winding up notice. There may also be other small companies you will take down if you don't pay them – then their receivers will be after you.

You could deal with the problem in this sequence:

(a) how much money do you expect to receive this month?

(b) how much of your overdraft facility is unused.

(c) use spare overdraft plus the first of the incoming money for the payroll.

(d) use the next money to come in for people you have to pay.

(e) the next is for people from whom you need supplies.

(f) the next is to pay as many small debts as possible – it gets them off your back.

(g) Then across the board payments to as many debts as possible.

Month 6 – Expected receipts – £600,000. Present overdraft balance – £400,000. Limit -£600,000. (£200,000 spare overdraft facility)

Outstanding balance at beginning of period:

(a) Payroll estimate £150,000

(b) People you have to pay £100,000

(c) People you need supplies from £700,000, of which £300,000 are due in a month

(d) Small debts £500,000 (117 companies of which £400,000 overdue)

(e) Other debts £1,300,000 (20 companies all over 90 days)

Next month you expect to collect less cash than this month, so pay:

(a)   £150,000

(b)   £100,000

(c)   £300,000

(d)   £30,000 (twenty companies off list)

(e)   £100,000 (all get something)

So your closing overdraft is £480,000. As the next month is likely to be worse, this leaves a survival margin. The closing balance of small debts is £470,000. £400,000 was overdue. £400,000 is STILL overdue. You paid £30,000 but another £30,000 became overdue.

Other debts, £1,200,000. You still have twenty very angry companies, but at least they have received some money.

REMEMBER, IF THE BUSINESS DOES COLLAPSE, THEN:

(a)   Any assets will probably be taken by financial institutions covered by fixed and floating charges on bank loans/overdrafts.

(b)   Next, the preferential creditors get paid, which in the U.K. is the VAT, Income Tax, National Insurance.

(c)   What is left, which is likely to be very little, will go to the people having the first legal claim.

(d)   The remainder will get nothing.

When you tell people the company is –

- legally trading
- paying everybody as soon and as fairly as possible
- expecting to clear all the debts

- they have the right to take legal action, in which case they will probably get nothing

– most people will be reasonable. SOME ARE NOT. This is why it pays to start reducing the large debts to something more reasonable. Thus, if one goes to a winding up notice you can possibly cover it. In other countries, it depends on the legal situation.

- In one company in Saudi Arabia, I never did know exactly what we owed. Every month a new debt would come out of the woodwork which I knew nothing about, ruining all cash flow projections and planning. In the case of a foreign company branch failing, i.e. going bankrupt, the senior foreigner went to jail.

- In Iran, on a major construction site, the money for payroll, contractors and local suppliers, used to come wrapped in newspaper – OVER ONE MILLION DOLLARS! I initially tried to reduce the backlog of ex-employees who were owed their pay-offs. So, in my supposedly organised English way, I nominated one day a week every week and paid them. Then everybody who was behind with their wages started to quit. To stop the work coming to a halt, we again changed policy. First, we now paid the site payroll, sub-contractors and necessary suppliers, and then started to pay off back-money to ex-employees and sub contractors. Some people would come 150 miles seeking payment. Then they would offer to take 90% in full settlement because they didn't want to come again. Moral dilemma. We decided to pay them 90% and donate the balance to a Muslim or Christian charity depending on their religion, when we next had money.

- In Greece there was a wonderful firm of consulting engineers. All debts were paid at the due time at the end of the month. It was fantastic – and it worked.

Those accountants who think that their job is not to pay

people when they have funds, especially in large companies in the UK, are in my opinion, guilty of moral fraud. They are not accountants, but confidence tricksters.

I really need this money, this is the twentieth time I've phoned.

Let Little x wait another four weeks for payment.

Conclusion

Be truthful. It often hurts, but it is better than a pack of lies.

CHAPTER SEVEN

Staff – The Most Valuable Resource

There is no limit to what people can do. In all companies, in all departments, there are people who, given the opportunity, will shine. Of all the resources you possess when you take over, it is the employees who can most help to turn a business round quickly, or send it crashing to its doom.

In this chapter we will look at what people can do. The next chapter looks at some of their more negative aspects.

Initial stages

In a struggling company you will find a lot of people working – and working hard – on tasks that add nothing to profitability or efficiency.

- In Iran, on a massive construction site, one part-qualified Pakistani accountant's job was to ensure that meals were signed for, and to keep the cost receipts for catering. I assured him that his job was safe, then moved him to the stores putting in systems and controls and later on doing payroll cost analysis. His stores work saved thousands in the first week. The job of meal recording went to an under-utilised clerk and our efficient part-qualified account continued to do all the actual catering accounting work.

- In Greece, I had just taken over a department. I needed to look at a lot of costs and systems quickly. After cleaning up some of the more basic tasks, I needed to delegate the work. As a cost constraint I could not hire; indeed, I expected to reduce staff once we had re-organised. In the office was a sixteen-year-old girl fluent in four languages, who, at the whim of a director, was photocopying every

73

cost invoice (sometimes several times) and filing them under each applicable cost code. Since nobody ever referred to these filing cabinets of photocopies, I stopped it. As a result, in the next six months, £20,000 was saved from costs. In addition, two members of staff were not required. A job costing was successfully introduced, and all the cost of the unneeded photocopying was saved.

Explain the position and tell the truth

Obvious – but rarely done.

As soon as you possibly can, tell those people whom you need to keep, that their jobs are secure for 'X' months whilst the turnround is taking place. In many cases, they will want this in writing. This means identifying key people at all levels. It also usually means dealing directly with them, which will cause organisational problems. These problems you will have to live with. You need as many people as possible with a positive attitude. There is nothing like insecurity for causing good people to leave their jobs – and it will be the good people who will go, i.e. the ones who can easily get jobs because their skills are in demand or because people know of their abilities and approach them.

Particularly important are those people who can sort out units/departments and make them efficient along your guidelines. At the end of the exercise they will have often worked themselves out of a job. They need to have it spelled out well in advance that this could be the case, but that they will then have the opportunity to go on to greater things. SAY IT CONVINCINGLY – AND MEAN IT. If you cannot say it, give them a financial incentive which they can work to.

Training

Vitally important if done properly. Continuous, small

amounts are the most effective. Even in the short-term, some non-formal training can have major effects on cash flow and profitability, in that order.

The following suggestions are by no means exhaustive:

In the Factory or on the Construction Site.

(a) Less use of power: equipment should not be left switched on when not needed.

(b) Better working practices. This includes safety training. Safe workers are happy and productive workers. When shown a better way, people will follow it and often make a better suggestion. Also, consider the negative effects on morale and production of serious accidents.

> One Monday morning a man fell under a press and it made a terrible mess of him. There was virtually no production that week in that department.

(c) Better planning even at its simplest, can avoid equipment being hired for longer than necessary, or stocks being built up through purchasing materials too soon. It can drastically reduce work in progress. Concentrating on getting work out of the factory – not just departments – can improve cash flow by giving priority to those jobs which produce the most net positive cash flow.

(d) Material specifications. What does your customer require? Are you over-engineering?

(e) Getting the operations people to contribute to marketing: they have a lot to offer.

(f) Understanding why higher costs in production can lead to higher profits.

(g) Making savings by bringing the shop floor into production planning.

(h) Investigating inspection procedures. A good craftsman should be able to inspect his own work and put his name on it.

The Sales Force

(a) Make them understand that motion and action do not equal profitability. Planning and desk research have their very necessary place.

(b) Improve training in letter-writing and use of the telephone. Many companies ignore telephone sales.

Note: Highly expensive courses at luxury hotels are not always the best value. One of the best courses on selling is a three-hour evening course held at different locations throughout the U.K. Even very experienced salesmen will get something from it. Payback can be in hours rather than months or years. The most important factor is the fuelling of enthusiasm

The Despatch Department

(a) Make sure staff are completing documents correctly and that documents are used properly and not lost: this avoids non-payment and ensures that any insurance claims are valid.

(b) Selection of carriers – cheapest is not always best.

Office Environment

(a) Don't type everything out, or automatically photocopy it.

(b) Proper use of the telephone. This includes obtaining information from callers, and using cost effective techniques.

(c)   Check that staff understand how each service is charged so they know what it costs, and can make sensible decisions based on value and cost.

(d)   Use staff efficiently: a secretary with twenty years experience can contribute more to the company than dialling calls for a twenty-five-year old high flyer. The secretary's expenses and skills could be used to organise the office and paperwork of production management, releasing both their time for technical work and saving the company thousands of pounds through increased efficiency.

Motivation

For some people money is the sole motivation. For others it might be opportunity, praise, promotion, status or even fear. It is no use your motivating people if some senior staff in the organisation are negative-minded; they will undermine your efforts. If people are working their best for the company and an executive pulls rank, perhaps demanding that a member of staff to do some mundane or even personal task, then you must take action. The first time it happens, warn the offender – in writing. The second time, give the warning in front of the staff. The third time, fire him.

Bad habits and staff potential

Good habits (working practices) have to be learnt. In my experience, the staff with the greatest potential are:

(a)   Youngsters. They expect to work. Especially those who have just completed some tough exams requiring self-discipline and personal study, and those with few or no qualifications who want the opportunity to work.

77

(b) Married women over 35. Especially those returning to work after having brought up children. The best 50% of this group are the best workers and the most cost-effective people I have come across in the U.K.

(c) The cynics. These have been pointing out for months and years what is wrong. If they honestly believe you intend to turn the company round, they will be your best workers. Remember, they have often a good knowledge of your company. They can point out the problem areas before you find them.

Reward

In the turnround situation there are no rules. You want to survive. You can worry about precedents later. Use small bonuses or treats. If necessary, use large or even enormous incentives if that ensures survival.

Suggestion scheme/prizes

If your company already has one, liven it up. If not create one; for example:

'Cost saving idea of the week', 'Best sale by non-salesperson' etc. Whatever you can think of – let the creative juices flow. Whilst you are at it, have competitions for improvements in efficiency and profitability; for example: safety awards, individual and teams; 'Cleanest van' (if you believe this is a key image); 'Most improved worker/timekeeper'; 'Production group with least rejected goods'; 'Salesperson with greatest contribution to profitability (note – not sales); 'Salesperson converting largest number of cold calls into sales' etc.

This sort of thing is so much better than using men with clipperboards and stop watches. There are very few production or clerical tasks that the people actually doing the job cannot, if motivated, organise better than outsiders.

Status

Yes, it is important to some people. If those people are junior production or sales staff, then it is important to you! If they have the confidence of their group and can lead from the front, then that is exactly what you need. It may well be that an effective salesman works on his own. The same could be true of a skilled engineer or craftsman. Just because somebody tells people what to do, this doesn't make his status and reward necessarily higher.

Why people insist on promoting first class salespeople into third rate sales directors puzzles me.

> A young and first class speciality salesperson was bringing in over £100,000 contribution (not turnover) above his own cost. As a sales director he cost £70,000 more and wasted £40,000 on ill-conceived and badly executed ideas. He upset customers, potential customers and staff, AND SOLD NOTHING. Value of this promotion to the company – MINUS £210,000.

Once you have promoted staff, you cannot easily return them to whence they came. So, if people crave status,and they are achieving required performance, give it to them within the cost budget. Don't increase your base costs beyond what is reasonable. A promotional trip, a course, a one-off high reward may be right.

Try not to be too status-conscious yourself. Why not use a car that is not too flashy, or use a car from pool? Why should you have a special parking place? Why not turn up early or walk!

Do away with executive dining rooms – except if you entertain customers – and I don't mean people who will buy from you anyway and/or would rather go out for a meal. Have an area of the canteen cleaned up if you are at a factory site. Perhaps have your own table roped off. Every day invite some of the junior executives, foremen, shop floor workers to sit with you. Once they get used to this procedure and start talking, you will learn a lot. It is good to have one or two people at the table who can get the conversation going. You relax and listen. Don't make notes during the meal – surely you have a memory?

Dial your own calls. Go on the road with a salesperson, or a delivery driver. Turn up early one morning in a set of overalls and spend the morning in the factory. Do the same with the night shift. Don't always wear a tie in a department or industry which doesn't like them.

Turn up at branch offices unannounced and then insist staff just get on with what they are doing. Stay in a reasonably-priced hotel. For your lunch, on an expense claim, regularly have a sandwich. Handwrite memos. If your handwriting is poor, practice in your own time. Sit by the switchboard and help open the mail sometimes.

Co-ordinators

Some projects need a co-ordinator but he/she should have some specific task as well.

One man was always busily involved co-ordinating his team with the clients, the other three firms of consultants and his own directors. He organised meetings, briefings, and engaged in communication. They went on a training exercise. A team of six had to build a cut-out castle. No status here, just a need to get it done. As well as planning, everybody had to work, and work together. Not our man. He touched neither scissors, cardboard or glue – and it was glaringly apparent, even to the senior partner. After half an hour the senior partner told him either to pull his weight or leave the team.

Lines of command (span of control etc.)

It is amazing the amount of time people spend drawing up organisation charts, including those with dotted lines (these show non-formal lines of authority/reporting). The best one I ever saw recorded the production, sales, and essential clerical tasks in the middle of a circle, with support departments next and with the board of directors on the outer rim. An organisation chart is a guide. Often, even with dotted lines, it does not indicate either authority or control.

You can often see it in school. One teacher is no more senior than the others, yet when he or she tells the pupils to do something, it will be done. Other teachers can never get the actions carried out as quickly or to the same degree or same efficiency. Through personality, or the respect generated, that particular teacher has the real authority.

Earlier in this chapter I advised you to confirm to certain members of staff that their personal future is good for 'X' months. Once you have made that decision, tell the member's manager and work though him – if you are keeping him, too. Continue to maintain contact and ask questions and opinions, but don't remove the employee from one task to another without getting the manager's agreement. After all, you are expecting this man to organise his staff to get agreed results.

Flexibility

In a company which is fighting to survive, people have to be willing to do tasks that are not in their job description. The most useful people when you first start are those who will do whatever is needed. They may not do each task as well as others could, but they get it done immediately.

Amongst the new arrivals at a company in Saudi Arabia, was a self-taught cook. He was also an ex-Royal Marine, member of the SAS and goodness knows what else. Whilst others waiting to be allocated to distant construction sites were sitting in the sun, this man was willing to help – he just hated being idle. When we were short of a purchaser, he helped out purchasing. Off he would go with his provisional licence driving a truck all over the city.

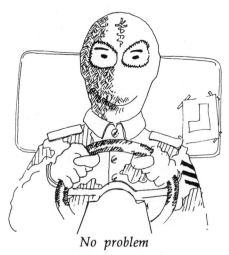

No problem

When he came back to tie up his receipts, there was always more cash than there should be. Discounts were given in cash, but nobody else had ever come back with any. If a truck needed unloading he would be on it doing the work. If we needed to pay people off at another location, or deliver supplies, he was always willing. Eventually, for logistics, he was kept at the main location – I never did find out it he could cook! During the time I knew him, 70% of the UK workforce was replaced, but never flexible Peter, he was just too useful.

Final comments

1) Lead (and I mean lead, not order) from the front.

2) If you are wrong, admit it. Once you do, others will follow.

3) Whatever went wrong, concentrate on avoiding it in the future, not on covering your back or blaming others.

4) If you are genuinely interested in people, they will know it. People work well when they believe what they are doing is important.

5) Give praise for work well done or special effort.

6) Eliminate negative people, especially those in senior positions who de-motivate others.

7) Be a person people can talk with in confidence.

8) Encourage healthy competition and team spirit, but respect the solitary individual who is making a solid contribution.

9) Encourage ideas and taking initiative.

There is no limit to what people can do with encouragement – Helen Keller springs to mind.

CHAPTER EIGHT

How to fire people – quickly, cleanly and painlessly for both parties

Unless you are in a most unusual turnround situation, you will need to remove employees. Don't get too God-like, my friend, because at the end of the turnround it is often time to remove you: you will have made yourself reduntant.

Who do you remove?
When do you remove them?
Whose advice do you follow?

Oh! if it was possible to find a straightforward formula!

Start with the non-executive directors. Unless they are the ones who insisted on the turnround, remove the lot. Their job was to be independent.

The people you may need to remove will fall into several categories:

(a) the incompetent

(b) the lazy and idle who cannot be made more efficient

(c) people whose skill specialisms do not justify keeping either them or their position full time in the present circumstances

(d) the dishonest – the more senior, the faster

(e) people who are just excess to requirements

Honesty

There is a need to be honest. Tell the staff and unions that you believe the company can be turned round and can prosper. Tell them if there is to be short-time working and what they can do to help. If people are to go, try and work within agreed procedures and remove those who will face the least personal upheaval. Don't just go for voluntary redundancies – this way you often lose all the best people and those with transferable skills.

Who is most important

Production? Sales? Management?

Remember, the factory employees are as important to your survival, if not more so, than many of the administrative staff, and both are usually more important than the present management. Much time and effort is often spent agonising over the future of certain very senior and incompetent employees. These people are left in positions of authority where they undermine other peoples' efforts to turn the company round. They are negative and pull rank. All it does is to discourage the good people in the organisation, and produce the reaction: 'Old Fred is still here. I don't think he's ever going to go. All this talk of change is so much hot air.'

Action

1) Fire somebody as senior as possible, by the agreed and legal procedures. This makes it clear that there are going to be changes.

2) Find a good commercial solicitor (or lawyer) who can tell you the relevant procedures required. Do not use the personnel department. Hiring and firing is a line manager's function. A personnel department is a staff department. In a badly run company or division, the

personnel function comes to regard itself as a charity being funded by the company. Once the company is sorted out, get a good personnel manager. This person should be able to fire anybody cleanly. He/she should also be able to come up with potential recruits when required and should be able to try to match skill requirements with what is available. Many of the best people in specialist areas usually go off and set up their own companies.

3)   Inform members of staff about their jobs. Whether they be factory manager or cleaner, make it clear that their jobs are definitely good for, say, the six months of the turnround, as long as performance is kept up.

4)   Deal with those people whose skills are only required, or can be afforded part of the time. Tell them the truth: that you value what they do, but you cannot utilise them all of the time. Very often, these people may have already been thinking about going into business for themselves. You can then give them some guaranteed

initial work. So we have the best of both worlds: you are getting work done at a fair cost and your ex-employee is better utilising his skills in his own business, with a guaranteed initial client – you.

5) Go through the company with a vengeance. You need somebody to produce the goods and services; somebody to deliver; somebody to service, if equipment is involved; and somebody to calculate wages, pay suppliers and collect from customers. All of these need to be looked at for their staffing levels. All other departments need to face some short questions.

Hold the following discussions with department managers

Question: 'Does this department add value to the company?'

Answer: 'Yes'

Question: 'How much?'

Answer: Perhaps a figure which is the starting point for investigation, for instance, how calculated, assumptions, which costs are included etc. More likely, you will get 'It is difficult or impossible to quantify.'

(Note: Be very alarmed if you get answers which involve words such as 'prestige', 'corporate responsibility', 'synergy', etc.)

You should then explain that tomorrow evening you want a handwritten sheet showing person by person how the manager could reduce his/her department in size, starting with the first person to remove. Insist that they show the effect of the reduction how it can be carried out and how the company would cope.

Accept no excuses for not carrying this out. From the lists produced you will see how each of the managers see their departments fitting into the business and how they rate their staff. Good managers will often put themselves on the list well before the last of their staff.

Next day, with the manager, call in all the under managers and give them twenty-four hours to do the same exercise. They are not to consult with each other, nor their manager. Anybody who is asked to do so is to come to you immediately.

The quicker you can remove as much dead wood as possible, the better. The organisation is slimmed down and gets to work, rather than playing politics.

Cash constraints

You cannot always remove who you want, when you want. You have cash constraints.

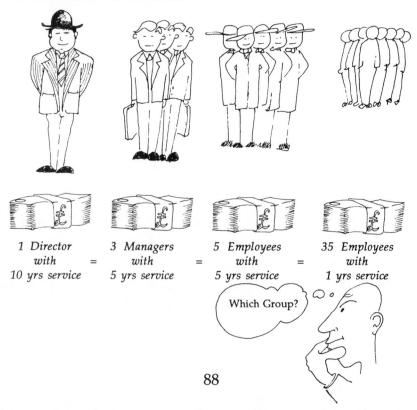

| 1 Director with 10 yrs service | = | 3 Managers with 5 yrs service | = | 5 Employees with 5 yrs service | = | 35 Employees with 1 yrs service |

Which Group?

Whilst running an operation in Saudi Arabia and another in Iran, my company could only spend what money was collected or was allowed from Head Office. Some people had multiples of weeks due to them in service benefits – sometimes a year's salary. However, the company also paying for their vehicles, accommodation and often food as well.

My first action was to attack the problem from both ends – one senior manager out, plus a group of new labourers out. You only see the benefits in cash flow terms of your reductions in the third or fourth month after you have taken action.

The trouble with this creeping reduction is that it causes everybody to become unsettled. Some people, if you agree to a date of leaving, will work flat out to that date because you have taken them into your trust. Others will cease to do anything or become deliberately destructive. Slowly the work force shrinks. At certain times, dismissals stop. Is this the end, you may think? The answer may be yes, or perhaps that you cannot afford any extra from the cash flow. At the end of the exercise you will probably be the most unpopular person in the company, even though you have slimmed it to profitability. Your reward will most certainly be, in an overseas context, transfer or dismissal. This improves morale which your successor can build on.

Bear in mind that the cash flow costs of a person are far more than direct salary and benefits.

(a) If your manager has a company vehicle, he will use it. You thus have fuel and maintenance outgoings. Can you sell the car or buy out the lease? For what?

(b) Your manager will have other expenses paid for by the company – hotels, books, courses etc. It will be interesting to see what. Many employees are very generous with their company's money, but expect them to pay out of their own pockets for a change, and you see a different story. The very generous become incredibly mean.

(c) Your manager will be using the telephone, usually inefficiently. He also has staff. This does not mean if you remove the manager, you remove the secretary – who may be the best you have. It does mean that you must have under-utilised resources. Thus, a junior manager in a marketing department could well have a direct cash flow cost to you, four times as much as a factory manager of twenty years service.

I have always noted that people who bend over backwards to help managers being terminated, don't give five minutes consideration to junior staff, and even less to those on the shop floor. This is because they identify with the managers and are afraid of being next.

Don'ts which will save you money

1) Don't just accept verbal agreements or written agreements of staff/employee contracts. Just before you take over, get your commercial solicitor working on them.

2) Don't accept staffing levels. See what can be done. Ask the team directly. Get a commitment. If you make promises, stick to them.

3) Don't reinforce demarcation of jobs. Who says a van driver cannot sell? Who says the switchboard operator cannot collect cash?

4) Don't be impressed with qualifications. It's what people can do, not what certificates they have that matters. Why all this graduate recruitment? In my opinion, this equates to stereotyping and lazy recruitment!

5) Don't believe that people on the present staff cannot manage a department just because they have no experience.

   During the time I was working for an airfreight company, offices would have between six and thirty staff. It always amazed me how, when somebody left, a senior clerk would take over the position of the number two manager, plus his or her present work. Lots of people can manage. Few are given the opportunity.

6) Don't throw a lot of money around on ex gratia and other extra or unjustified payments. The money is not yours. If you have such surplus funds it is better to spend them on motivating staff.

7) Don't believe that managers shouldn't work as well as manage.

8) Don't be vindictive. Some of the people leaving will go to your customers. An ex-employee should be able to say about being fired, 'I didn't like the experience, but at least he/she was fair.'

9) Don't go for a standard percentage reduction of all departments. That is not being 'fair', it is avoiding responsibility. You are being paid to manage. The best you can expect is to be respected for your tough decisions. You are certainly not going to be liked.

   Manager A always keeps his numbers down and efficiency up; Manager B is a chronic over-staffer. If you apply a standard reduction, Department A will cease to function and the manager will leave. Department B might now be down to reasonable staff, but the manager will never run it effectively and now he has another reason for non or poor performance.

10) Don't plan factory or office moves based on your own or your spouse's prejudices as to where you want to live.

A southern service company with a very weak accounting department took over a northern company with a very lean accounting department. The northern department was closed. Result – cheap, efficient workers were replaced with temporary staff, costing four times as much. Mistakes were made and a well-controlled positive cash flow became negative.

11) Don't believe that a policy of last in, first out is best. It badly skews the age range in the company and leads to complacency by those with longer service. You also need to be practical. You cannot, in the short-term, remove a newly hired welder in order to keep a purchaser with more years of experience – the skills are not transferable. This also leads to another usually ignored area of difficulty: at the same time as slimming the organisation, you may need to add people to certain functions, and in 'no new hiring, and first in last out' agreements, this is impossible. You will also need to bear in mind that the type of people who justify being hired at such a time, will be very good – and attracting them from secure, well paid jobs to a run-down company will not be easy. Whatever you do, be truthful.

A factory manager aged about thirty, had risen, from an initial position on the shop floor, through four companies, during which time he had developed into a very efficient worker. Approached by an outsider, he was offered the chance of a higher salary, better car and the prospect of a directorship within two years. The manager was very impressed with the company's new factory, order book, products in the pipeline and eventually agreed to the offer. However, he was not told of the company's appauling financial position; so when he joined, he found himself continually debt collecting and short of materials and equipment. He used his own contacts to get supplies and then they were not paid. His car took three months to materialise. As well as his other duties, he was given the responsibility of completing the factory; and as a result of poor design work by the managing director, this was no easy task. Six months later and very bitter, he left the company to set up his own buisness in a low cost area – in direct competition.

Employee benefit changes

This is a crucial area of morale and costs. Once people have been granted a benefit, it is difficult to remove it or replace it with a lesser benefit. In a straight take over you can offer new contracts of employment with the new benefits. This solves the legalistic, but not the morale problems. You can always freeze benefits for new employees or newly promoted – the 'what they've never had, they'll never miss' theory – but this is only a temporary solution and will have to be dealt with more fully when the company is afloat again. I believe in knowing the true cost per employee: if a member of staff has been granted a benefit, take it into account when reviewing the salaries. Given a straight choice of cash or benefit, you soon realise which benefits are:

(a) wanted by the employee irrespective of monetary value
(b) adding to costs and having no positive effect.

Temporary and third party staff

This includes contract workers, who are usually believed to be more expensive – but are they? This is an arguement that is often used to protect permanant staff and fails to take all employee costs into consideration with temporary staff it is easy to add to or reduce capacity. Some of the temps will be looking for full-time jobs, so you get a chance to test work with them first. Others will be 'permanent' temps and among them you will find both your worst and best workers: the worst because companies will have hired X number of bodies at Y rate, so everyone, regardless of performance, is paid equally; the best who value their independence and are involved in many different activities – which is why they became contract workers in the first place.

In addition, your cash flow is often more favourable.

How often do you come across the company which has an open early retirement or redundancy scheme? Many companies pay off key workers and then end up re-hiring them as temporary workers!

Re-hiring

In a closed community, job opportunities are few and far between. If you have had to rationalise your company, a possible counter-policy is to have people made redundant the first to be re-hired. In principle this is fair, but only if the reduntant person really is the best candidate for the job – his/her previous service will be the final deciding point.

Conclusion

Firing people is never a pleasant subject. If you have to reduce staff for the company to survive, you should remember that losing 20% of staff is better than 100%. In addition, if your company fails, many of your suppliers' staff will also lose their jobs: just as companies support each other, when one goes down, it may take others with it.

The most important points are:

(a) Remove those people, functions or departments not required by the business and do not apply blanket methods over the whole company.

(b) Be as fair as is possible. Treat people as you would wish to be treated in the same circumstances.

CHAPTER NINE

Get out of the Accounts Department – your job is to use information, not produce it

RUN THE ACCOUNTS DEPARTMENT AS A PROFIT CENTRE – NOT AS A COST CENTRE!

Remember:

- Finance departments should be run on the basis of aiming to contribute enough to at least break even.

- Finance should be a profit centre and not a cost centre. My favourite story is of a board meeting in a northern company where the finance director was stopped mid-sentence by the chairman and told he had no right to comment as he was just a 'bean counter'.

Although this chapter is aimed mainly at people with a financial background, be they accountants, bankers, business graduates or whatever, the three main points are:

1) People are employed to produce information. You can question –

    - the information

    - the basis on which it is drawn up

    - its accuracy

You don't produce information yourself just because you have a financial background. If you decide you want a cash flow on a daily basis for next year, that is what the accountant should produce.

2) A certain amount of formal work has to be done in an accounting department, and if the staff genuinely have limited resources, then asking for one extra report or piece of information, will delay another.

3) You have been employed to turn a business round and not to engage in your original discipline, no matter if you can do that particular job better than anybody else in the organisation. You will often see –

   - engineers doing drawing board work
   - production engineers who spend all their time in the factory
   - salespeople concentrating on turnover, not profit
   - marketing people concentrating on market share, not profit
   - ex-auditors concentrating on financial accounts, not on the management accounts and cash flow
   - ex- 'people' people rewriting the staff handbook

However, it remains true that the worst offenders in turnround situations are financial people. Often appointed by the bank or the holding company or straight from a large consultancy, they have a tendency to feel more comfortable in the accounts department than any other.

Auditing has its purpose, and can be an extremely useful discipline for a company; but it is not a training for running businesses in trouble where you need to be able to think on your feet and motivate people.

Reports

1) Why people still insist on typed reports I will never know. They take longer and are often not as accurate as handwritten ones. Typing is also less confidential.

2) As information moves through and up an organisation, it becomes 'sanitised': what starts off as an unimportant task for a production worker with a blunt pencil writing on the back of an envelope is, by the time it hits the holding company, typed up on pretty paper and reverently presented in a bound folder.

3) Ensure that reports circulating are necessary and useful. How?

    (a) Stop them being produced – see if anybody notices.

    (b) Add a paragraph of complete nonsense – see if anybody questions it.

4) Information gets stale very quickly.

    Remember that 95% accurate today, is BETTER than 100% accurate in 2 weeks time.

5) Often it is the trends that are important, not the finite amounts.

6) In the turnround situation, unless it is required for a bank or for statutory purposes, any information that

cannot be used to improve the company's performance is worthless. You do not have the luxury of either dwelling on the past or apportioning blame. Get to work – you have a company to turn round.

7) Do not forget that there are other important items to measure besides money. These will often lead to greater profit; for example: staff utilisation reports, percentage distribution for a retail product, product awareness, customer complaints per product by reason. The particular figures depend on your particular business. Don't just ignore them in favour of financial information.

8) If you have a time waster: a writer of countless useless and time-consuming memos, organiser of meetings, co-ordinator for this and that – FIRE HIM. Nothing gets the message home faster that staff are there to work, not to play politics.

9) The supreme test of any report is to give it the 'so what?' test – 'So what do you suggest we do? If nothing, why are you wasting my time with this information?'

CHAPTER TEN

Salespeople/Agents – A necessary nuisance

You may be able to do everything else right, but WITHOUT SALES THERE IS NO BUSINESS. Sales are the life force of a company. Without sales you cannot obtain cash.

O.K., point accepted, but let's look a little further. Sales do not always mean profits (see Chapter Twenty). In the turnround situation, some sales are the turning into cash of a slow or non-moving stock or underutilised assets. Or you may just be unloading goods for cash, which you are desperate for. Neither of these are policies which can continue for too long. Eventually the business has to become profitable.

A sale is where you get paid. Any fool can 'sell' goods to people who never pay for them. Many salesmen seem to forget about the sale once it is booked.

Here you are, the company is a mess. Perhaps you are not selling enough, or perhaps you are selling too much at the wrong prices. Given any group of people, salespeople included, some will be doing better than others. Why?

For the answer, I suggest you ask first the sales director/manager and then the salesperson. In the next week, talk with each salesperson individually for about three hours. Get him/her to open up to you. Each will have something to contribute.

Next, look at sales management. Good salespeople don't necessarily make good sales managers; and you don't need prima donnas and information collators in the sales force. In the short-term, try sending back all the sales staff, including the director, to actual selling. This need not be on the road selling; staff could use the telephone to call prospects and

100

make appointments; they could send out mailshots, or research past customers or possible new ones from trade directories.

Before putting this fantastic effort into sales though, do make sure you can produce and deliver the goods. Hopefully you will have a few product costings by this time to ensure you are not selling at a loss.

Next, look at commissions. Only pay them out when the company receives its money. Otherwise, for the time being, leave the system alone – unless it is to enforce special short-term incentives.

Are the salesmen selling? Sounds obvious, but you will often find the taking of orders, and even the selling is carried out by other members of staff, the salespeople taking the credit because it is 'their customer' in 'their territory', or whatever.

Does your salesforce sell? In some companies, representatives will be sent out to visit customers and take orders. Can some of this be done by 'phone, or by other people? Could more products be sold to these customers while the opportunity is there? What are the actual, or expected skills of the salespeople? Are you in a cold call industry? Could somebody make appointments rather than a salesperson personally cold calling?

What is the personal motivation of your salespeople? Is it that:

(a) at their age it is the only job that comes with a car?

(b) they like travelling?

(c) they want eventually to get off the road into sales management?– or change function completely? – it is surprising how many buyers started out as sales reps.

(d) the overall package is good and commission on top useful?

(e) it's better than being in an office/factory etc?

(f) they can control their own destiny, make a lot of money?

(g) they can easily arrange to meet their friends?

So you say we need (f) above. Yes, if the skills match the motivation and you are in a one-off sale per customer rather than repeat business. It could be very difficult if your salesperson did not understand that service also leads to repeats. You often see this where a specialty salesperson gets a management role in a repeat business company. He/she jumps on leads, upsets present customers and has usually been promoted out of the position before the real problems come home to roost.

Another problem is the theory that being on the road is the most effective work. It is not. One-to-one contact with a decision maker is what you want. Ten phone calls are better than driving 330 miles to one customer, unless, of course, that is the only way to close him and the business is profitable.

1 sales call today.

Ten sales calls today.

In many companies the status of salespeople is low and the grumbles in other departments are familiar:

Production   – 'They just don't sell enough of what we produce.'

Accounts   – 'Always spending a fortune on expenses and never putting in correctly completed expense claims.'

Distribution – 'Always giving free delivery. How they find some of these remote companies, I don't know.'

Interestingly, it is often marketing departments that have the greatest contempt for salespeople. I remember an outside lecturer at business school talking about teaching evening classes in marketing to salespeople – 'The only skill they have is how to hang their jackets on hangers in the back of their cars.'

It is very easy to criticise salespeople – but go out and try it.

This can be very hard, energy-draining work. You will be on the receiving end of all sorts of sarcasm: all faults, actual and imagined, of your company and its products are your fault. Appointments will be broken or you will be left waiting – to hell with your schedule for the day. You will rarely get offered a drink (and I mean coffee). 'Oh, it might be nice to get out of the office or factory,' you say – try it, every day . . . in winter . . . when it is raining . . . when you don't feel great!

Probably the recruitment process has a lot to do with it: the advert which says – 'No experience required. Fantastic product. Leads. £30,000 in first year. Unlimited commission.' – newspapers seem to be full of them. Perhaps that tells us something.

What about the interview? – Well, tests, of which I have been on the receiving end, include:

(i)

(ii) 'How many rungs on the ladder showing?'

Was this ship's ladder test really useful for somebody going to sell edible oil to fish and chip shops?

The actual question was:

A ship has a twenty meter ladder. The rungs are one meter apart. It is now four p.m. and the tide is out. At five p.m. it will start to come back at two meters per hour. At the moment fifteen rungs are above the water. How many will there be at ten p.m?

[For non-salespeople, the answer appears at the end of the chapter.]

I think both tests demonstrate the problem. There is a presumption from the public and the media that a salesperson has to be smooth-talking and calculating. Yet, in fact, the most successful are often quiet, thoughtful people. Also, a huge importance is placed on appearance, but you can overdress!

One of the best courses I ever attended summed it up:

- People buy people first and benefits second.
- People buy benefits, not products.

Right, back to action. You have found the above fascinating and have now decided what type of salespeople you need for your organisation. At the very top (i.e. effective) are those who are self-employed agents or work on commission only with no limits. They are certainly not attracted to struggling companies – they don't need to be: they are in demand. As a result, your salespeople may be of poor quality, poor product knowledge, low self-confidence, and disillusioned.

Let anybody in the organisation who seems to have selling potential, for example, good product knowledge, confidence, willingness to take some training etc., go out and try it.

Next, hold an extensive telesales campaign on past customers. Any information these can give you is worth having, even if it is only to list your faults.

If you are in the appropriate kind of industry – hold a seminar. Don't spend a fortune, but any interesting subject should get some potential customers in to listen.

What about self-employed salespeople and agents?

One theory says you cannot control these: they are disloyal. How loyal is your present sales team? Within reason (as long as no trade secrets are given away) what have you to lose? Be careful, though. There are a lot of self-styled salespeople out there, and just starting a self-employed one will take the input of some valuable time and resources.

Evaluating a salesperson's performance.

Oh, I have seen all the ways!

- Route planning charts
- Number of cold calls

- Number of calls
- Sales by value
- Sales by units, etc., etc.

It all comes down to being subjective. If you are not satisfied with a salesperson, out he goes. YES, fire him/her! Be careful, though. At the beginning, it might be better to keep on any salesperson whose added value to the company from sales covers his/her total cost, or anyone producing a positive cash flow.

Try to encourage your salesforce.

1) Go out on the road with one and ensure that all your other senior executives from other disciplines, especially finance, do this too.

2) Encourage written reports from salespeople, not reams of garbage, but short pieces of information. These people should actually be out daily in the market place.

3) Get salespeople to set their own targets. They are likely to be more committed to them. If in your opinion the targets are reasonable, accept them. Don't become target blind. The person going for a tough target who misses it by 40% is often better than the man going for the easier target who exceeds it by 10%.

4) With those who need a strong hand, tell them after a frank talk: 'You achieve X in Y months or you have to go.'

5) Invest some training money in the sales force. No, not big hotels with expensive meals and booze-ups, but small courses on, for example:

- Effective negotiation
- Telephone training

- Short managerial psychology courses
- Role playing
- Use of video for feedback

Ask staff members what they think they need to improve their performance. Put them together every so often (say once a fortnight/month) and get a good open discussion going.

Commission

You are trying to survive; you therefore need cash flow, and sales are the only continuing method of producing it. Do understand how the commission system works for all sales.

I have seen sales at less than cost; free delivery not costed in; commissions paid on despatch of goods and not payment of account; systems with no deduction of commission for returns and cancelled goods/contracts. I have also seen salespeople paid commission on annual maintenance revenues they had done nothing to originate. Under no circumstances should commission be paid to the salesperson until his/her employer is paid by the customer.

Agents

Review quickly the commercial aspect of all present agreements with agents. Then have a legal check made. It is surprising how little of the arrangements is written down. You may also find your files are incomplete, whilst the agent is in possession of an up-to-date position! Ask yourself the following questions:

- Do your accounting records tell you the full truth of the relationship?

- Does the agent have competing agencies?

- What problems has the agent had in the past?

- How does the agent's performance compare with other agents?

- How does it compare with your own salesforce?

- Go and visit your agents and see what their operation is like. (For overseas agents, see overseas operations.)

- What are the cash flow arrangements?

- Can they be improved by trading off some profit?

Territories

These depend on your operation. A territory should be expected to have the potential to achieve a certain volume of business after a certain time. Before making an area exclusive, enforce some target figures on it – and review them after a period of time.

Finally

Don't move competent salespeople into management. You often do not get management and you only end up losing whatever they were contributing to profit/cash flow.

> A top saleswoman was bringing in £100,000 over her costs. Within two years she was a director of a subsidiary. Her cost was now £60,000 and she was bringing in no sales. The company was £160,000 WORSE OFF.

If some of your salespeople start earning fantastic amounts of commission with the system you have set up, whether through effort or luck, don't decide to change the system or to enforce a limit on it. You need this business and you need to encourage others with the prospect of what they will get if they make similar achievements.

Solution to Ship's Ladder Puzzle:

There is no change as the depth of water does not effect the ship's displacement. In simple terms, the ship floats, so the same number of rungs (fifteen) will show irrespective of the change in water depth.

CHAPTER ELEVEN

Stock – The Quagmire – What is it worth?

Stock is a component of working capital. If it is not being regularly sold for cash, IT IS NOT WORKING.

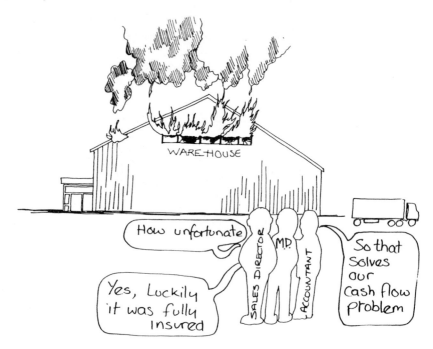

The above is the time-honoured method, probably still widely practised, for solving the problems of:

(a) Turning non-moving stock into cash.

(b) Losing what you don't have. This is probably not the method you will consider as it is clearly criminal. However, the principle of turning slow moving stock into cash is vitally important in the turnround situation.

1) Ask yourself some key questions regarding stock:

   A) What do you have?

   B) Where is it?

   C) What is it worth?

A) What do you have?

   (a) Quantity

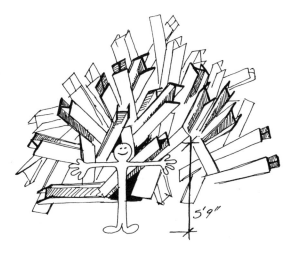

The man in the photograph is 5'9"

A massive construction site in Iran – to give an idea how massive, the smallest of the four main projects was for thirty tower blocks of office accommodation and supporting services and buildings, for example, shops, schools, etc; in fact, the site must have been well over one hundred square miles in size.

Upon arrival I found that there were no stock records. Members of staff just did not know what they had or where it was; and, driving around the site, it was quite common to come across large piles of girders or steel plate, reinforcing bars and other materials.

So I organised a meeting followed by a stocktake of the total area. All the counting was done by building foremen, superintendants and surveyors. Each area was drawn into grids. A further team checked that there was a list for each material pile in each grid in its area. Quantity surveyors then calculated quantities, qualities and value. Amongst the stocktaking returns were three photographs stuck together with sellotape in the form of a montage. Depicted in the distance of this montage were the mountains; in the mid-distance, buildings, dwarfed by an enormous pile, mainly of steel; and in the front stood a stocktaker. Attached to the picture were the immortal words: 'The man in the photograph is five feet, nine inches tall.' On the basis of his height, a quantity surveyor (trained by experience, and not just qualifications) estimated that there were 20,000 tonnes of steel pictured in the photograph. This figure was ridiculed by the site manager, so the surveyor checked his figures and found he had put in an extra 'zero'. Still, that was still 2,000 tonnes: some of it good to use for its original purpose; some could be utilised for other purposes; the balance was scrap. Oh yes, the man in the photograph, even with heels, was not an inch over five feet, six inches. So what did we actually have, and what was it worth? Six months later, these stock sheets were still being used by the construction staff to allocate materials.

(b) Quality

This was recorded in the books as 'soap powder' stock, priced at the current production price. As is usual with all interesting items, it was right at the back of the stores. Following up certain hints from the storeman, I checked the stores records and discovered that it had been there a long time; indeed, it was from an old sub-standard batch. Nobody wanted to take a loss by writing it off, and recently it had been moving slowly but surely. So the old material of a different mix was being mixed in with the new wonder product. A fortune in marketing support, including special advertising was being spent. Without the knowledge of the London-based product manager and marketing staff, the factory was mixing in a little old stock and eliminating its problem. At what risk to the business?

B) Where is it?

Oh yes, but you have a computerised stock control system, nice computer printed stock sheets, or even on-line information. I'm always suspicious of computer generated stock records. To find out why, go back to the starting point of many stock records on the factory floor – usually bits of paper written with blunt pencils. Auditors mainly spot check using statistical sampling techniques. An XYZ blow out converter inlet value £250,000. If there is something in the stores which is claimed to be the blow out converter, down will go the tick on the sheets. This is especially true if it was in the same place last year and/or the same people are doing the stock audit. The fact that the items seldom move does not alert people. Many spares, by nature of their intended use, seldom move. Watch out for a new spare being taken from stock and the defective being left in its place. It is not always done deliberately, but it does happen.

The further away you get from your actual stocks, the neater the figures get. The only way to check what is there IS TO LOOK YOURSELF. A good regular walk round will uncover all sorts of items not listed or whose value is not appreciated.

C) What is it worth now?

An item is worth what someone will pay for it.

Certain items are easier to price than others. *The Financial Times* will give you a good guide for prices of scrap metal and other commodities. You also need to be careful of that other classic case – turning slow/non-moving stock into non-paying debtors.

> Whenever it is decided to reduce the stock, your most incompetent director or manager gets a list of slow or non-moving items. Why he needs this list puzzles me. Many of the items listed are the results of his own inefficiencies! List in hand, he rushes off to XYZ Manufacturing. They are a major customer who don't pay their bills, and are always complaining. Back he comes with a cheque for a proportion of the old debt, and having found reasons for raising credit notes for a high proportion of the rest. Lo and behold, at a bargain price (with no paperwork) he has sold £X worth of non-moving stock.
>
> You have nothing to celebrate. The effect on your cash flow is negative. You have moved stock to debtors and as your customer will not pay, you have added the payment of VAT output tax to your financial problems.

2) Look at the different components of stock individually.

(a) Raw materials

As these are not processed, they are often easier to sell. Do you use them? If so, how much is required? Is it worth keeping the excess? What condition are they in, for example, does the cement go solid if kept in damp conditions. Do they rust, rot, crack, etc.

(b) Bought-in components

This is a major problem area as these have an original cost and tend to be kept in the books at that price. Often they are specific only for certain products and if obsolete, are worthless (in conventional trading terms).

(c) Maintenance

In many cases, in a maintenance business, items will have gone out to replace a defective item – which then comes back into stock. Engineers are hoarders. You don't know what works and what doesn't – neither do they.

Engineer's nut hoard

Even in a true maintenance business, little real work is done to calculate by stock value the level of stocks needed for the customer base. This could be based on common sense, experience, or simple mathematical techniques.

There are great opportunities in maintenance as a continuing source of revenue and positive cash flow. Decide what you are going to support and when you will stop providing maintenance support. Also, have your legal paperwork drawn up by a competent commercial solicitor.

(d) Electrical and computer spares

These can go down in value incredibly quickly and can become obsolete even faster. Just because technology has moved on does not mean that these items do not have a value, especially if you or your customers have expensive partially-depreciated kit to support.

(e) Semi-processed goods

See chapter on 'Work in Progress'. Often this stock is of the least value as it requires more expense to put it into a saleable state.

(f) Finished goods

Here your opportunities are largest, but you have to be careful.

(a) Staff sales and a factory shop can always move a certain proportion of excess stock, usually at no worse margin than wholesale, but you can usually only move small quantities.

(b) Can you move stock directly to new wholesalers with or without re-labelling or re-branding? Make sure this has no adverse effect on your present distribution chain; it is no use selling 20% more to 'A' if you lose 30% of the business to 'B'.

(c) Mail Order – possibly through specialist magazines, or nationwide or local press. Certainly in the U.K.'s national newspapers, if in your advert you ask people to send money (God forbid!) you have to belong to a mail order trade group. In addition to the reams of references, it has the usual structure of the smallest relative fees for the biggest advertisers. If you don't join, you cannot have what are the most effective cash raising adverts in the national press.

(d) Brokers can be effective, but as usual, there are some absolute rogues out there. Deal for cash or cleared cheque: until you have the funds, don't part with the goods. Market traders, if you can find and deal with them directly, are a good distribution channel for excess stock.

(e) Look for non-traditional distribution networks. This could lead to opportunities in the future.

I prefer to try to move stock by non-traditional methods which don't effect present business. It may be possible to get your present outlets to take stock early, or more stock for a one-off discount. However, beware of possible repercussions on follow-up sales and pricing.

Seller: 'How much do you want?'

Buyer: 'Oh, our normal 1000 cases.'

Seller: 'As you can see from the catalogue (writing order), we have again not increased our prices.'

Buyer: 'Oh yes, price! You now give us a special price that is not in your catalogue.'

Buyers start at the lowest price listed, or one they have achieved before. The fact that the previous bargain price was a special offer is ignored.

3) What is your stock worth later?

Sometimes stocks can be worth far more than book value when they are eventually sold.

- I was exhibiting at a new small business section at a county show. On the next stand were some beautiful silk goods. However, the stand's best selling product was squares of polyester at £1.00 each. These had been carried at nil value after a fire. Enough of these squares were sold both to pay the cost for the whole stand's worth and to make a profit. In addition, some solid leads were obtained for future sale of the silk goods.

- A company had all sorts of metal in its yard, including old cast iron wall plates and lamp posts. Lying outside in puddles of muddy water and covered in rust, nothing ever looked more like scrap metal!. The value in the books was written down to nil. The company adamantly refused to sell them off for scrap, although it needed any cash it could get. Every so often, an order would come from out of the blue. Staff would take an old lamp post, fill in any holes, sandblast it clean and paint it. Any fittings required would, if necessary, be manufactured. Out would go a high value product. What had been rusting scrap had become of significant value to the company.

- A group had a division making metal communication tubes for industry, of various shapes and sizes. Vast stocks were available which covered every system the group had ever made. Thus, when something wore out, as many as fifteen years later, people would re-order. What were the tubes worth? For financial accounting purposes the lower of cost and market value. As the orders were irregular they were carried on the balance sheet at virtually nothing. There was no knowing when there would be order. When there was, the pricing was farcical – historic price plus a percentage for profit. Inflation was ignored and not even an assessment of what the customer was prepared to pay.

The solution was easy:

(a) To stop manufacturing batches of spares. When an order did come in, sub-contract as necessary, often inter-group, and charge a profitable price. It was the design drawings which were crucial.

(b) Offer the present old stocks direct to customers as spares to be owned by them – at market price. If necessary, you will still store them at your premises and charge rent.

(c) Release warehouse space in North London and carry all present spare tubes in a cheaper site acquired in the Midlands.

- A multi-national company which has large operations in both the developed and developing worlds. A list of spare

119

plant available is circulated, ranging from individual machines to complete factories. Due to a technological change, for example, the European company has to replace its old plastics plant for a new one, it has its original plant written down to virtually nil. For a company in Africa, three times this book value is a bargain. The multi-national organises the finances, so the company in Africa gets a working plant and the technology. It is immediately ahead in its market. The European company gets a price of over twice the book value and so makes a profit.

You are unlikely to be turning round an operation of this size, but the principle remains true. Items which are not worth much to your company can be worth a lot to others. You have to find them.

Supposing you have in stock certain old, technically obsolete items. Their book value is written down to nil. Then suddenly, due to their age and rarity, they gain value, for example, old street lamps, telephone boxes, etc.

Government taxes can distort a product's value. In the U.K. we have excise duty on wine. You could have a stock of wine which is duty paid, which the owner is offering to sell for less than the cost of the duty. Why?

You cannot reclaim the duty – it is a sunk cost.

4) Associated costs of storage/stock holding

A) The most obvious cost is space:

  (a) Do you rent space for excess, non-moving, or slow moving stock?

  (b) Do you rent other space which could be released if you could move items into (a)?

  (c) Could you sell or lease back such space?

(d) What insurance costs could you save if you release space?

(e) Security costs, for example, you have fifty cases of whisky in your grocery warehouse. You cannot sell it easily, but if you give it away, it would go tomorrow. Thieves rather than vandals will come for whisky, but have no interest in your cornflakes, etc. It may pay to give the whisky away and fire the security guard!

(f) Heating (or chilling). Do you have some products requiring this, but others which don't?

B) Record keeping

Reduce the quantity and number of stock items, and the bills should come down for:

- staff costs
- computer time
- audit costs – there will (or should be) a big reduction if you remove lots of contentious, slow moving and obsolete items.

C) Money, i.e. interest

If you have an overdraft or loan, then any stock you can turn into cash will save you X% (i.e. your borrowing rate). If your funds are positive, you can use this extra cash in the business or invest it on the money market.

D) Management time

This needs to be used in areas which will make money for the company. Discussions with banks, auditors, etc. on stock values don't make your business one penny, centime or dime!

5) The costs of selling stock.

If it is dead stock, look at the difference in strict cash flow terms. What cash will you receive? What cash will go out? This should tell you the incremental cash flow. Don't forget to look at when the cash flows take place.

A) Transport costs

(a) You may have to move the stock to your buyers, for which they may or may not pay.

(b) If you have your own transport, you may incur overtime costs.

(c) Don't let anything leave without checking that any necessary material handling equipment will be available at the other end.

(d) Ensure the receipt and the despatch paperwork is correct, and that you have P.O.D. (proof of delivery).

B) Goods in transit insurance

Where required, but only for the amounts not covered by common law.

C) Commissions to brokers, agents, your salesforce/staff

In case of special stock clearance (even if not standard company practice) these should get paid only when you get paid. Also, any staff payments should go through the proper P.A.Y.E. scheme.

D) Further processing

This may be as simple as fettling or painting. It may include packing. With chemical products, further processing either at your own or other peoples' premises may be required.

E) Advertising

This also includes any costs for producing special lists of items available, and mailing them.

F) Financing costs

How can there be any? Well, depending on the timescale of your transactions and the payments received, you may have corporate, sales or other taxes to pay before you are paid.

G) Time

Look at the lost opportunity cost of your employees and managers normal jobs – if it is nil, perhaps you are carrying excess staff!

6) The balance sheet value of your stocks

How important an element of your balance sheet is your stock?

A) If the stock value is holding up the balance sheet whilst you are cleaning up the company, then if you sell it off and find its true value you may:

(a) Find you are technically insolvent

(b) Remove crucial asset cover from your financing arrangements.

It always surprises me how little real business knowledge bankers possess! Why they concentrate on assets, particularly land and buildings, as opposed to current operational cashflow which is the key to business turnround, I do not know.

If a company needs turning round, then it has probably been badly run. 'Oh,' you say, 'it could be sudden technical change', but a board of directors is there to think ahead, i.e. to think strategically.

B) If the company has been badly run by financial accounting people, then you could have a serious problem of vastly overvalued stocks and work in progress, etc. It if has been run by salespeople, engineers or operational financial people, there is some hope. With these people, many stocks and assets will not have been recorded – what will their value be?

An engineering company was living literally from day to day with a massive overdraft. A complete stocktake of the factory was organised and supervised. Everything was counted, every box and tin investigated. It was an industry where people visited sites or maintained machine; items were 'won' and 'lost'. As a result of the stock take the value of nuts, bolts, washers, etc. was increased from £1000 to £35,000. It was there, it could be physically verified.

The design people were told to incorporate as many of the excess fixings as possible into new jobs. Fixings did not need to be bought for months, in some cases years. In addition £30,000 worth of other non-moving stock items could be sold for cash.

7) Scrap

What an emotive word. You need to have worked in a

jobbing engineering works or in construction to realise how little material really is scrap, i.e. of no value.

Let's look at some interesting sub sections.

A)   Off-Cuts

This could be metal, wood, cloth, plastic, rubber etc, and is an area with a great deal of potential for saving, increasing profit or both.

In Stoke in the early 1970s, the staff and I were installing a costing system. Off-cuts lay all over the factory. I was having people make up standard product sheets mainly for the labour and component costs. As I was including the standard plates from which the items were cut, I asked who decided what could be cut from which size type of plate. Nobody did! It was discovered that we could cut other basic components' shapes out of the off-cuts, and thus save another 10%. Previously all plate off-cuts went off to the melts or scrap merchant.

Usually with new products in manufacturing industries, a price is quoted, and the actual materials and labour used are recorded and used for future pricing. The people manufacturing the objects are technically challenged and if they think of finance they think of cost savings.

Thus, this off-cut and that off-cut in the production area is used to make the new product and not recorded. Result – when an order for a hundred goods comes in, the actual materials and labour are recorded as used, and the company makes a loss – which gets larger as sales of the item increase.

B)   Waste

Waste is exactly what it says. It is of no value. In fact, it actually costs money in that it has to be taken it away and even processed.

How to have removed for free, a table which is worthless

Wrong *Correct*

C) Traditional Metal Scrap

In other words, a pile of metal of different types, including off-cuts. Note that this may be worth more in its constituent parts than in total. How?

- During my training period, I spent a couple of days with a clerk at Derby Railway Works. The clerk had many duties, only one of which was scrap sales, a very small part of his work. He used to put in unbelievable effort to protect his employer's interest. Oh, to find such an employee! However hard the contractors tried to organise a wagon-load or more of mixed scrap at the lowest price and the most profit potential; our man would refuse to give in. The wagon would be re-sorted to extract copper, aluminium, brass and lead, metals which had prices of up to thirty times higher than was being offered for the job lot.

- You remember the huge pile of scrap metal on the Iranian construction site? In that we discovered many beams in perfect usable condition; others plates and beams of useful sizes could be cut from the twisted pieces; and valuable copper, aluminium and reinforcing bars were extracted. Eventually, when used and sold, the pile returned five times the value awarded it as general scrap metal.

D) Other Scrap

Think creatively about what you have lying around your factory floor – it can lead to new products. I come from a town with a large number of skilled workers; and what they could produce with bits of scrap was amazing: fencing, car accessories, name plates, bird houses, etc., etc.

Other suggestions:

(a) Boilers can be run on wood off-cuts.

(b) Pallets which lie around all factories have a market price. Few firms seem to bother about recovering these.

(c) Waste paper: if you have sufficient, contractors will buy it; if not, it can go into the boiler. The backs of computer print-outs make excellent cheap scrap pads.

(d) Old machines: non-required electronic components etc., can be sold to hobby shops, or to businesses which specialise in selling old parts, or to support kit which the major firms of the industry have written off as obsolete.

E) 'Second Hand Uses'

After being used for their original purpose, many items have other uses. Tea chests, for instance, are used in household removals and widely used for packing personal effects for international airfreight and shipping. This can give them a life of decades.

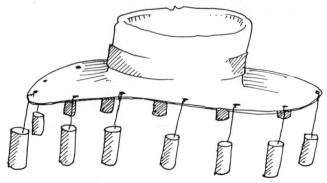

Excess Bottle Corks = Fly repeller

8)   Service Industry Stocks

These deserve a book to themselves. For instance:

(a)   If you don't fill the pre-paid seat on today's plane, it is lost forever: you cannot use it again.

(b)   Ditto, room seven in the hotel tonight.

(c)   Ditto, the quarter page of advertising space in this month's magazine.

Revenue gone forever.

The main problem here is to make sure that any discounting does not take away a contribution from a person paying full price for the service; for example, holiday companies have bargains late in the season, so people book later and later. Eventually, they never bother booking early, they just wait for the late offers.

9) Office Stocks

These are usually counted as part of the overhead and then ignored.

- How much money do you waste on unnecessary stationery?

- How many times do staff use embossed letterhead paper as scrap?

- Why does virtually everything go first class mail?

- Why can't people just write a note – why does it have to be typed?

- Do you monitor small portable items such as stapling machines, hole punches, filing trays? I have often taken over a desk and found maybe twenty pens, pencils, erasers, etc. left in it. Multiply that by the size of your company.

10) Final Points

Most of what you generally read about under stock control, I will cover under purchasing. In this chapter I have concentrated only on the movement and financial aspects of present stock holdings.

Often one comes across excessive stocks being held by companies which are very short of money. Some of these stocks may have been bought in because they were offered at a bargain price. Great, if you are going to use them. Stupid if you are not. Beware of false economy! One of the main reasons for this attitude is that separate profit centres don't get charged for their stock holding costs. They simply go to the general overheads.

> In Riyadh, when we were continually short of money, one of our engineers managed to buy at a very cheap price (20% discount) five years supply of refrigerator compressors!

Do you actually own your stock? This is not as crazy a question as it might seem. Just because it is on your premises does not mean you have title to the goods.

It may be possible to return some excess stock to the original suppliers, though much depends on:

(a) What it is.

(b) How long you have had it.

(c) How much potential future business you have for it.

(d) What the discount figure is, if any.

For a positive decision about what to do with it, go as high as possible in the supplier organisation.

Finally, a word about three techniques widely written about in textbooks.

(a) Materials requirements planning 'a commonsense technique' of working out what you need from orders received or planned production.

(b) Kanban: just in time manufacturing. Can you forecast this well? What about your suppliers (and in order for it to work, this means all your major suppliers) – can they be trusted? It may be perfect for profitable and/or large companies who can impose and will to achieve efficient supply.

(c) Statistical stock control can be a disaster, particularly when operated in less than perfect circumstances, by people who don't think about what they are doing.

- You clear some old stock and, horror of horrors, because it has moved, more is automatically repurchased or manufactured.

- A market is drastically changing and yet you keep carrying much higher stocks than justified on forecasted future business. Not only that but you don't start to clear them when it would still have been reasonably easy to move it.

CHAPTER TWELVE

Manage your Bankers – and other professionals

Why do companies who will negotiate their suppliers down to the last penny and refuse to pay their staff overtime, never query an undetailed professional's bill for thousands of pounds?

Yes, there are some first class professionals out there who will save their fee many times over. So they should! Otherwise why are you employing them?

There are far too many audit firms who issue bills for extra accounting work which nobody has authorised and nobody has itemised; banks who add extra non-agreed charges to accounts; consulting engineers who charge for extra days on site caused by their own negligent design, etc., etc.

Always insist on having an itemised bill – however much this offends – unless the work was a complete assignment at an agreed price. If, when you receive the detail you are still not satisfied, ask for a further breakdown into people, time and expense categories.

If you need or can use a first class professional in a particular area in a turnround situation, then it makes a great deal of sense to use a third party. That way you should make or save more than the cost of the original fee. You don't add to your cost base and you should get a better quality of worker, or at least a more committed one, than if you had to take the time to recruit your own employee – always supposing you could recruit the right person. A potential employee is unlikely to be available for usually two to three months and it is now that you need this service.

Solicitors

A first class commercial solicitor is essential. You need somebody who can, and will, give simple verbal replies over the desk and on the phone: somebody who gives you practical advice in language you can understand and who understands the relationship of that advice to your business; not somebody who is preoccupied with legal jargon and status. A good commercial solicitor is hard to find. For example, you may have to ask him/her questions such as:

(a) What can happen if I break this contract?

(b) How do I get rid of this employee?

(c) What is my liability under the lease?

(d) What will it cost to take this case through each stage of possible legal action? What are your estimates of the percentage chances of winning? What is my potential liability if I lose?

(e) How can we change some of our practices to improve our right to being paid, and protect title to our goods.

Few solicitors seem able to talk to the layman and also be highly competent at crossing the 'T's and dotting the 'I's. You are much more likely to find good commercial legal advice in city centre practices than from the local solicitor, who is often a divorce or house transfer specialist. Some local legal firms can be very inflexible, very expensive, and remarkably ignorant with regard to business. They can also be very slow and commercially naive. As we all know, trying to sue them or get compensation, though supposedly possible, virtually never happens. If your company is in trouble and you have received poor legal advice, sure, you may eventually get compensation; but by then the damage has been done and your company will probably be in liquidation.

> Going into his own business, a friend of mine wrote to a high street local solicitor, suggesting they held a half hour getting-to-know-you session, and that a meeting out of normal business hours would be most convenient. Back came a reply that a minimum charge would be made of £50 plus VAT per hour, payable in advance. After receipt of the cheque, an appointment could not be made for at least three weeks, and then only during the morning. A city centre solicitor, on the other hand, gave my friend his half hour free and picked up over £20,000 in fees in the first year.

Audit (accounting) firms

Why should firms just accept audit fees and extra work bills? If you are in trouble and you change auditors, the bank will often stop supporting you. You don't have to be ripped off, though – insist on a written quotation. Auditors can make life utterly miserable for accounting staff. Working flat out to keep the company afloat, they do not appreciate somebody two years out of qualification/university, who has never run a business, scoring points at their expense. Remember, if your accounting staff leave you, recruiting others in the short-term will prove all but impossible.

A good hard audit, on the other hand, conducted well and to budget is useful: it is an independent check with fresh and unbiased eyes. I am astonished when particularly small audit firms suddenly decide they have the experience to produce management accounts for small firms. Many small businesses don't feel they have much choice, or knowledge of alternative producers of accounts.

There is a lot to be said for employing an independent management accounting firm. These people want your firm to survive. Their speciality is information to manage your business with.

Another great waste of money is the auditors' recommendations on the business or systems – the so-called 'management report'. If you don't want it, don't have it. If they say it is free, it means that it comes under the overall audit cost. Tell them to reduce the bill. Another extra you usually don't want is a 'source and application of funds' statement. Use the same principle to reduce your bill. 'Ho', you say, 'it could be useful!' WRONG!! Go back and re-read Chapter Two. What happened in the year ending three, six or twelve months in the past is of no importance to present cash flow!

Another tactic is for the auditors, in the case of a financially weak company, to drag their work out until the end of the next financial year. You get the signed audit for the year ending 31/12/89 on 2/1/91. Auditors are in the clear: the company lasted a year after the period the signed audit report is for!

Remember, your company is not there to train your auditors. Many large audit firms' junior staff seem to have no knowledge of double entry bookkeeping or commercial accounting, and train at your expense. When you've got the company going the right way i.e. partially turned round (and the financial institutions will allow you a free hand), look at the level of your audit cost and ancillary fees. Compare these costs with other companies' published accounts. This can be an eye opener. Doing the exercise at one company, it was discovered that the audit fee had dropped from £83,000 in 1983 to £10,000 in 1988 – and no difference in the quality of the work. In the later year the auditors just got on with their job under a strict time limit and cost budget, and overall there was less disruption of the work to the accounting staff.

Banks

1) International Division

> Banker: 'Yes, let me lend you £ billion so that you can pay the interest on your present loans.'

> Mexican: 'Si, Signor, but the interest on all previous loans now to be less. Reduce from sixteen percent to twelve percent.'

> Banker: 'Yes, we can accept that.' (meaning that 'all the loans to you in my balance sheet stay as assets because you are paying the interest.')

2) Local Branch

> Bank Manager: 'You will have to manage your affairs better. You cannot have unauthorised overdrafts of £300.'

> Customer: 'It was due to our Mexican sale of £3000 not being paid on time. What about the request for a loan of £5000 to buy an XYZ machine?'

Banks always look after good payers!?

Bank Manager: 'No loan. I am now increasing the interest rate on the whole overdraft of £4,000. From three percent over base to six percent over base. We bankers have to protect our shareholders' funds.'

I always remember working for one particular company in Saudi Arabia – it was a financial disaster. It kept issuing letters of credit for more stock, despite the fact that present stock wasn't being sold; and bid bonds for potential new projects when it could not manage the present ones. Every time we went over loan facility limits, I as financial manager, had to go down to the bank to be reprimanded, even though I was not signing the documents.

On his next flying visit to the country our chairman would visit the bank and inevitably he would negotiate yet another increase in the facility. When I was leaving the company, I asked him how managed it. His reply? 'They are in too far.'

Try to get a good relationship with your present banker/s. If the local manager is just unhelpful, then go over his head. You need to survive.

Supply your branch manager with monthly budgeted and actual management accounts and cash flow, in confidence. As soon as you possibly can, start building a relationship with another bank. Then you can negotiate with one and use your relationship with the other as a lever, i.e. play one off against the other.

I have heard of cases involving people who have drastically improved the position of a company, only to have the bank call in the loan – why ?

	Starting Position	Six Months Later
Assets	1,000,000	1,000,000
Liabilities	1,000,000	350,000

Assets: If forced sale, will realise £500,000. Only £5,000 of assets is in cash.

Assets: If forced sale, will realise £700,000. If sold as ongoing business will raise £1 million.

Bank owed: £600,000
Bank will continue to support.

Bank owed: £500,000
Now they foreclose.

This is because:

(a) They do not believe there will be much further improvement in the financial health of the business.

(b) They want their money out, plus accrued interest while they can be sure they will get it.

Bank Managers are there to make money. They are NOT superior or God-like creatures.

Years ago, a friend of mine was going down to the bank to:

(a) open an overseas account

(b) take out some life assurance, and

(c) give power of attorney to his father.

He was dressed quite casually when he went to collect his father, but the latter was in his best suit ready for the occasion. You may not have this attitude, but many of your staff probably have.

The right bank manager can be very useful. He will have a good contact base, and banks can provide a lot of optional information free.

Remember, banks are in business to make money. Indeed, your manager probably works through profit share schemes or commission. Watch for the following:

(a) You are granted a loan on which you pay, say, 16% and are expected to keep a proportion in an account at 0-5% interest. Crazy.

(b) Your outgoing cheques always get cleared first. Incoming money always seems to get to the account the day after a large amount of outgoing cheques have been cleared.

(c) What is the interest rate being charged? How much is that over base rate? What do you have to do to reduce the rate you are being charged? How does the interest rate compare with what other companies are paying?

(d) What fees are you paying to run your account? Do you know? How is it calculated? Are they negotiable?

(e) Some companies have several accounts and pay interest on those which are overdrawn – whilst also having

139

funds which are sitting in non-interest accounts! This can sometimes happen at the same bank and even the same branch.

(f)   As soon as you can, get a facility organised rather than relying on an overdraft limit.

Property People (Consulting Engineers, Surveyors, Architects, Estate Agents)

In the turnround situation, you are most likely to require these people when:

(a)   you have partially completed buildings

(b)   you want to sell some of the land/buildings

(c)   you want to change the use you are making of land/buildings.

Get the fees quoted and have the work specified in advance. The more detail you have in writing about what work you are to receive and when, the easier it is to compare with what you really are receiving. Be very careful about who can sign for or approve extra work. You may not notice an increase in the builders activity until its too late to countermand one of your employees reckless and unnecessary instruction. Regular progress meetings with minutes taken by your people, circulated and approved, are essential.

Always know what you are committed for. If you don't understand the jargon ask – and continue to ask – until you do and are satisfied. In the case of these professionals, their fees are only a very small percentage of the cost of the work or projects they control. The cheapest service is not always the best value for money.

Risk Consultants (Plus Insurance People/Loss Adjusters)

Insurance brokers, salesmen etc. need to make a living, so somebody has to pay them. You will often find the following:

(a) Your company is grossly under-insured in certain areas.

– Usually in the areas that have, or are, giving you problems. You have limited funds. There are difficult decisions to make. If you take all the insurance recommended and required to cover all risks, you will probably go out of business – you cannot afford this and you don't have the cash. To some degree, business is about taking risks. You need to decide what to cover, and what excess you will accept. Then you have to live with the decision and continue to monitor the risk.

(b) Insurance is treated as an ongoing expense. Policies are automatically renewed. Increases are automatically accepted and no comparison with other company's policies is made. There is usually scope for some savings here.

Risk consultancy would appear to be a growing specialisation. If you have an insurance claim then as long as the consultants' initial fee is reasonable, you probably have little to lose. Loss assessors can often negotiate high compensation and save you a lot of time, as can arbitrators. If by using a specialist rather than going through the courts, you can get your money from your claim quicker, the savings will usually cover the fee. Remember to include the interest on money received earlier as a saving. It is also better value for money to be advised what to settle for, and be told exactly what the risks are for if you go for more.

Management Consultants

Management consultants exist in all shapes and sizes – from the one-man business to large international groups; from specialists to firms who claim to 'be able to do all things for all men'. It makes sense to use small independent firms. You can only afford to employ consultants who will work with and alongside yourself. Some of the large firms concentrate on producing reports which are of no use to you, especially the 'we think that you should consider/contemplate' type of report. Two classic 'prestige' C.V.s are outlined below:

Top Practice Consultant	Accounting Consultancy
1. Age thirty-two	1. Age 30
2. Public School	2. 'A' levels
3. University	3. Oxbridge
4. Short service commission (guards)	4. Auditor – four years to qualify
5. Banking – three years	5. Two years in industry, say in major industrial group. Special investigations, etc.
6. Two years manager in a Blue Chip (Leading U.K. Company) Head Office.	6. Returns to accounting firm as a Consultant.
7. Joins top consultancy	

If available, you need somebody who has worked at several different companies. Perhaps someone with some overseas experience, who has worked for firms you don't recognise. If he/she has been unemployed at some stage – perfect. A spell of unemployment makes people hungry for it not to happen again.

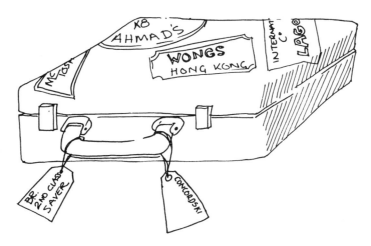

The consultant YOU need.

You need practical people. People with experience. The typical career consultant in a large firm is, to a large degree, a hand holder, or may have been called in as an insurance policy – to reinforce somebody else's opinion, or to save someone's making a decision for which he/she could be held responsible. Often often a consultant from a large practice will place great emphasis on methodology, and sees writing a report as the ultimate goal. In your situation you require people who can act.

Conclusion

Evaluate professional services as you would any other service.

Apply the same controls as for other purchasing.

A good professional should recover for you his/her fee several times over (this may be counted as cost savings or extra revenue). If this is not the case, why do you need him/her?

CHAPTER THIRTEEN

A

Production – What are the bottlenecks and cost constraints?

In some service industries, operations may be a better word than production. Such operations could be processing insurance claims, booking flights etc. Even if they are only to be performed by clerical staff, you will still need to calculate their productivity. Or you could be a delivery company where material handling is your operation. This chapter is aimed mainly at manufacturing companies, but some of the information will be of use for non-production companies.

Introduction

I spent twelve years working in and visiting many manufacturing units before a professor at business school finally explained to me something quite obvious (once you know it) and important, that I had never given any thought to: you either manufacture for stock or you manufacture to order. In practice, you will often find a mix of the two.

Fundamentals

Since in a previous chapter we have already dealt with the subject of stock, I shall largely ignore it here.

(a) What is the manufacturing capacity of your machinery, and sections in both machine hours and finished product?

(b) What are your manufacturing skills? Really! Do you have any?

(c) Do you have a list of the operations required to produce a schedule of materials required for each product?

In the days before mini-computers were in wide usage, at one company we carried this out manually, starting with the most commonly manufactured items in a product range of three thousand. I enquired as to how it was decided to cut out the metal, and then asked if there was a drawing to show the cuts from the different sizes of standard steel sheet. Nobody had ever actually formally thought about it. As a result there was a 20% saving in material. So, before you run off and buy a C.A.D. (Computer Aided Design) system, see what can be achieved by simpler methods first.

(d) How state-of-the-art is your machinery? Is it working? Do you have planned maintenance or do you just wait till machines break down and them repair them?

(e) Do your people go out to look for technically challenging, interesting work which is only marginally profitable, or even unprofitable?

A company had two types of work:

- Standard designs produced by third parties. Very few people worked on these, but the products were highly profitable.

- Contract work. State-of-the-art. No two jobs the same or similar. Even before allocating the cost of design staff, the work was at best only marginally profitable.

(f) Do you use standard components? Do you use industry standards? The 'not designed or made here' syndrome is a major problem. Why are you designing and manufacturing components that can be bought in? 'Oh', you say 'we have excess capacity.' Are you taking into account the cost of design time, special jigs, tools, and stock holding?

(g) In a manufacturing business, by far the largest amount of cost will be production related. I know this sounds, and is, obvious; but it is surprising how many manufacturing companies know the cost of their audit, but not of, say, reworking defective production or know the cost of electricity for heating/lighting, rather than powering machines. What are your significant costs? Even more important, what are your controllable costs? You don't know? Find out!

(h) Are you moving material either around the plant or between the plants unnecessarily? It is surprising what this can add to cost (and industrial injuries).

(i) Are you concentrating on production efficiency exclusively? Or the needs of the business? For instance:

- Do you see economic batch quantity or production efficiency as your key overall measure?

- If the sales department come in and ask for three of this colour, two of that, etc., do you complain that it ruins your production run time? Or do you celebrate? You should be aware of the costs of doing these specials and ensure that they are more than covered by the price. Also, you are building these items to order, not for stock.

- I come from what used to be a railway town. There is no doubt the old railway managers knew what their priorities were. Making a profit? No! Customer Service? No! It was keeping the trains running to timetable. This was why they always preferred freight traffic to passenger traffic.

(j) Do you know the lead times for your materials? Is there a forward production plan? Does it have flexibility built in? Really? Have you checked? How?

146

(k) Do you use sub-contractors? Has anybody looked into their efficiency/lead times? Do you really work with them, or is your purchasing department just oppressing them?

Quality

Probably you will have your people producing to the quality required and they will be looking to up-grade the quality where they can – this is fine as long as it gives you a competitive advantage and you can cover the cost.

A craftsman should inspect his own work. If he cannot, then he is some craftsman! Some factories are full of inspectors. What a crazy system! You promote your best production people into becoming checkers?

Scrap

Are you identifying why scrap is being created and where, in order that you can rectify it? Be careful: do you always rectify work when it could be cheaper to scrap? Sometimes it is.

Bottlenecks

Most of the original 'what if' and decision-making techniques were created for and used in production situations. The snag is that in theory you concentrate on one problem at a time, whereas in practice you may just be moving the problem on.

What is your limiting factor both as a production site, and within each production department? This could as easily be a shortage of labour, as a shortage of machine capacity; and it can radically differ between different production departments.

Once you remove one bottleneck, some other factor will overload the system. This new factor now becomes the limiting factor and potentially another bottleneck will be created. This is what is required, steady progress and improvement. In the manufacturing process, this is the area where I believe the Japanese excel.

	Y machine	Z machine	A machine	C machine
Units produced	10 per hr	5 per hr	6 per hr	10 per hr
You have	3 machines	3 machines	3 machines	1 machine
Hourly Capacity	30 units	15 units	18 units	10 units

Your starting situation is as above. C machine is your limiting factor.

(a) If you add one C machine, Z machine becomes the limiting factor.

(b) If next you add a Z machine, then A machine becomes the limiting factor.

Another type of bottleneck is the mental bottleneck, for instance, the resistance in many engineering companies to using plastics, which in certain circumstances could be as strong as, and lighter and cheaper than metal.

Efficiency Ratio

I much prefer these to pure work study. You need to get people working as a team. Many of the best ideas come from the shop floor. Efficiency ratios are one of the best methods of stimulating the workforce.

We once took an actual production department and told its members what we were doing in detail – we involved them. All

148

output, including part production, was valued in hours at the standard times for that work as set by the operators. The time of the employees making that production was recorded, less any time they looked idle or were utilised by another department. Where there were no standards at all, we worked on the basis of the number of units the production team could produce in a shift or a day.

It doesn't matter what the initial figures are, the improvements will come.

	WEEKS				
	1	2	3	4	5
Output hours	1000	1100	1050	980	1150
Input hours	1050	1050	1030	950	1000
Efficiency Ratio	95%	105%	102%	103%	115%

The labour hours fluctuate as staff are utilised elsewhere or become idle. The mixture of output can lead to different efficiency ratios, but these can be adjusted every three months. The team can manage themselves. This is a particularly effective method for assembly workers.

Remember that when you are using an imposed work study standard, particularly with a bonus or piecework element, then you encourage the skilled man to use his skills for himself, by maximising his income. WHY NOT?

In a firm which produced axles, the staff worked piecework. One worker had for several years produced at 200% efficiency on a scale where only 90% was expected and averaged. Occasionally his employers studied him (i.e. stood and watched him) but could not see why or how he achieved it. When he eventually retired, he explained to them that he had found if he machined a longer

149

standard bar than normally used, and cut it in the middle, he could produce two components. These were not to the exact standard size, but close enough to the tolerance to pass inspection.

Just think what effect that sort of mind could have on your business!

Idle Time

This is the responsibilty of management – not the worker. Yes – your responsibility!

A worker should be encouraged to record idle time. His company is wasting a major resource: its people's time. It also takes a lot of effort to get people to book idle time, but when they do, you can discover some important information. The system is best employed when reasons are also given: 'idle awaiting materials', 'idle awaiting fitter', 'idle awaiting tool setter'. You need to use some imagination and involve the shop floor in selecting the descriptions. They avoid inferring that they are simply lazy.

The results can be fantastic: better productivity, extra resource created, happy staff, less work in progress and more stock. Your formal manager will probably not put these systems in: he cannot understand why it should be beneficial for someone to say he is idle; if ever they did, the manager would probably fire him instead of seeking a productive solution.

Conclusion

Beware: don't get caught prioritising the flavour of the month, such as the time when everybody suddenly went energy conscious in the 1970s. This was all very good and commendable, but in production, no one item of cost is crucial to the continual exclusion of all others.

Recognise opportunities, like small savings.

At one factory, whilst helping to introduce a system, I moved from department to department with my factory expert, a brilliant young toolmaker called Barry. I would write down, with the agreement of everybody, the department's capacity. Not being technically-minded, I looked at the factory differently from everybody else. I asked different questions. Some were silly, many a waste of time, but some led to a new insight: in the paint spray section, four trays had been removed from the revolving system two years earlier and had been replaced with smaller trays. There were twenty trays in the system. Within a week the factory manager had the four small trays replaced. The improvement in productivity was 20%, and there was a similar saving in wasted paint.

Also large extra profits.

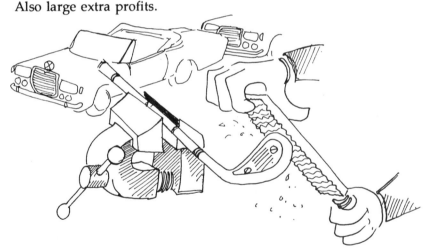

Why produce only cars when you can have Golf Clubs as well

A very skilled workforce was meeting productivity targets. No more material was being used than normal. Many of its men were earning good money and began to take up golf. Sets of golf clubs were expensive, and this was the type of town where nothing would be bought if it could be made for 'nothing'. So the workforce started producing the clubs at the factory. They were good clubs at a good price, and demand for them grew and grew. It wasn't until about two years later, that they were discovered by the management, and then it was only by accident.

Was the main instigator fired? No! He was put in charge of making the clubs on behalf of the company. A new product, and with no extra cost of production as the workforce had been absorbing the costs of producing the golf clubs for two years.

B

What are fixed assets?

If you look at your balance sheet you will see a written-down book value for fixed assets. What does this mean? Nothing. It is merely the original cost of something occasionally re-valued (usually property) with 'X' number of years of a theoretical life of use removed. Does it reflect the value? No – it could be more, is usually less and many assets will not be reflected atall.

Value also depends on use. A specialised jig or tool may have:

(a) Cost you £1,000

(b) Been depreciated down to £800 in your books.

(c) Cost £1,500 to be replace.

(d) In the case of your business closing, been valued as scrap at £30.

Adding assets

Capital appraisal techniques? Probably more books are written on this subject than any other. Why? Well, they give the academics the opportunity to use formulae and their mathematic skills and the banks will want to see some appraisal before committing their money; and it is intellectually satisfying. Discounted cash flow (D.C.F.) is quite useful as a framework around which to place your 'what ifs'. I still find it difficult to select the discounted rate.

What do most businessmen use, especially those using

their own money? Payback period? Perhaps if they could be encouraged to use discounted payback we would have a practical, useful and reasonably easy to understand technique. In the short-term, turn around payback in cash flow terms is all you can use.

Let's look at five potential projects

Investment

(a) £100,000   Will pay for itself in three years. All cash goes out in Year One. Decision – Shelve it.

(b) £500,000   Six year pay back, after which massive profits. Cash goes out equally over life of project. The cash flow in the first year is the same as in project (a) above. Decision – Shelve it, but put it at the top of the standby list.

(c) £10,000   Payback four weeks. Decision – What are you waiting for?

(d) £100,000   Payback six months. Decision – Maybe, depends on your exact cash flow.

(e) £1,000,000   Payback seven years. Decision – NO, stop dreaming!

I am always presuming that your company in this turnround situation is short of cash. In very rare cases, it could be cash rich: has just stopped investing and is in fact slowly liquidating itself.

Cash outflow

In the short to medium-term, this has to be your priority. Thus, leasing or hiring is preferable to outright purchase (unless you can negotiate some incredible terms).

Machine A	Total costs over the life of the machine		
	Lease	Hire	Buy
	£10,000	£8,000	£7,000

You can easily cover costs of the machine from its production for any of the above cost cash flows.

	Lease	Hire	Buy
Year 1	£4,000	£2,000	£7,000
Year 2	£3,000	£2,000	
Year 3	£2,000	£2,000	
Year 4	£1,000	£2,000	

So, on a one year basis, hiring is best. Leasing becomes equal with outright buy only at the end of Year Two, after which time you should be out of trouble, or out of business.

Why have I started by looking at increasing assets when surely we should be liquidating them? Well, that is the usual attitude, but a business should be worth more than its fixed assets as a going concern. All too often, purchasing (or leasing, or even hiring) of extra assets is stopped without having worked out its total effect on cash flows and the balance sheet.

We have four 'Z' machines working flat out. They produce ten units a day. All units have to be milled. Our two milling machines do eight units a day, so we have to work a double shift at premium labour rates. All production can be sold. The milling machine cost £15,000. Its capacity is twelve units per day.

We will initially only look at outright purchase, which is the worst on a cash flow basis, so if the investment looks good, we can examine the other financing methods.

The life of the machine is five years. Each unit adds £15 to profit.

Cash Outflow:

Year 1   £15,000

Cash In

Year 1	Number of Shifts	Total Contribution £	Contribution per Unit	Units	Operating weeks in a year	Years Life of machine
Extra production	1	41,400	15	x 12	x 46	x 5
"	2	68,000	less than double because of labour premium			

This is an extreme example, but makes the point.

Some assets are worth far less than book value

In the vehicle repair shops, due to a reorganisation, a company was having to have a vehicle inspection pit filled with concrete. One manager said quite seriously, 'It's a great pity: a lot of garages could really do with an inspection pit.' They could, but there was no way to move this one. It was, after all, a brick-lined hole in the ground. In the books the hole had a written-down value of a few hundred pounds, but obviously in these circumstances, this could not be realised.

Particularly in the case of office refurbishment, many costs are incurred which will have a use over one accounting period, and are capitalised. However, these assets have no, or virtually negligible value to a third party. Indeed, at the end of a lease you will often have to pay to return the premises to an agreed state of decoration and repair. I am thinking of such things as:

- Carpets
- Fabricated partitions
- Curtains
- Paintwork

156

My favourite example was having the cost of knocking down three walls capitalised. This was definitely a case of assets you could not see or ever realize.

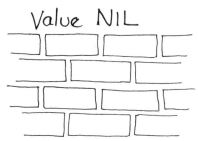

Tooling and jigs are capitalised. With jigs, particularly, if you stop making the part for which they are destined, their value is usually reduced to scrap only. With special tools, it is the manufacturing and purchasing costs that are capitalised. The research and design should have been costed, added to the total and depreciated over its useful life.

Another of my favourite examples of capitalisation is as follows: somebody had obviously made some very detailed calculations about a particular purchase of something which would have lasted more than one year in normal usage. The company had in its assets :

Factory	Several Hundred Machines	Office Furniture	and a Five Gallon can of Turpentine
£1,200,000	£2,500,000	£100,000	£3

The five gallon can is the wrong item. Once it had been capitalised nobody knows how to remove it from the books.

What do you actually own?

Consult the asset register if the company has one. You will often find it is incomplete, and well out-of-date. Without this it can mean the long slow procedure of having somebody go back through the accounting entries and invoices for six years. Even worse can be where the assets were included in a takeover. These may not have been individually listed, but lumpted in and have a group, rather than individual, value figure attached to them.

You may find you have assets on the company premises which have been acquired over the years. This is very common with contractors. With items you are leasing, make sure you don't sell them – it happens!

> One company had a fleet of cars financed by lease purchase. The company moved to a system of leasing under which it could never eventually own the vehicles. During a six month period the settlement figure on the leases was paid and the vehicles were sold off by the leasing company to third parties. The effect on both cash flow and on profit, was beneficial.

What monies do you still have to pay for your assets? In addition to the above, could there be hire purchase payments? Are any instalments of the purchase price due? Somebody may have a specific charge on assets (for example, the bank). You may or may not be able to sell them without permission.

What is the market value of assets?

Well, trade catalogues may be a guide but basically, an asset is worth what somebody is prepared to pay for it!

Turning non-used or under-utilised assets into cash

Obviously this is to your advantage. It must not however, become the sole objective: you are trying to turn the company round and not just liquidate it. In addition to outright sale you may be able to hire out equipment, but watch the insurance position.

Assets of no value

It used to be that companies would keep records of these, i.e. 100% written-down value, but I suspect that this is no longer the case for many. Some assets classed as 'no value' can actually have substantial values.

I don't see any way of purchasing the equipment we need.

A nationalised industry had taken over the many premises of previously private companies. Thirty years later, the premises and furniture were still in use. One of the internal consultants noticed a picture on the wall and had it valued for £80,000. How many old private companies still have such assets?

159

Assets in costing

Your prices are based on the market. You need to ensure that you are recovering the cost of your equipment so that you can replace it. This used to be a particular failing of U.K. companies. A machine would be written down to nil and so had no depreciation cost. It would then be included in the product pricing at nil cost. No funds were generated for replacing it and companies fell back in the international market place.

So try to use a replacement price in your costings. This can be very difficult, especially when there has been a change of technology, but it is no reason for not trying. A plastics company had one material 'X', priced to four decimal places of a £ sterling. At the same time, it ignored the difference in replacement and maintenance cost of tooling. All tooling costs were classed as overheads. Tooling cost ten times the price of material 'X' on some products, and thirty times on others.

> In Iran, the construction site on which I worked was three years old. Most of its services had been initially set up and then added to. We had the opportunity to sell oxygen from our plant to two third parties, and could claim the cost of repairing vehicles via insurance claims. This could include the cost of workshops, if we could prove it. So I did two things:
>
> (a) I had a quantity surveyor spend a day estimating materials required to construct the workshop.
>
> (b) Got a building foreman to estimate the labour required.
>
> We costed out and it came to a value – the cost of constructing a workshop – crude but effective.

Conclusion

Make sure you look at what assets you really have. Don't be fixed in your thinking.

Not seeing the wood for the trees.

- A firm had drivers road testing, basically truck chassis. As things frequently went wrong, they kept within a twenty mile radius of the factory: that way they could easily recover the drivers and vehicles. One winter's day, one of the drivers phoned up his co-workers at the firm, having walked half a mile to find a call box. 'Where are you'? he was asked. He looked out of the window and saw a sign which said 'DANGERSLOW'. Villages starting with 'Dan' and ending in 'low' were quite common in that area, but the maps weresearched in vain. Only when he phoned again four hours later, frozen stiff, did they realize which road he was on. They eventually found he and his vehicle next to a mud-splattered sign stating, 'DANGER! GO SLOW!'.

- Some men were taking up an unwanted spur of railway line. The line looped around a bend and was heavily overgrown. What was found around the final bend? – A railway engine. Four years previously it had broken down and had been shunted up the spur to keep the main line clear. Nobody had kept any records, and there it had stayed.

CHAPTER FOURTEEN

A

Sales – What are you really selling?

The Peter Drucker books give the best introduction to this. Twenty years after first reading them, they can still stimulate:

- Companies who thought they were in the railway, not the transport business.

- Companies who thought they were in the coal or oil business, not the energy business

- More recently, companies who thought they were in telephone, photocopying, computer businesses, etc. Now they find they are in the information business.

So what industries do you think you are in? Ask your executives and managers their opinions and estimates of:

(a) What your market share in each industry is, by geographic area.

(b) Market share based on units or sales value, or what?

(c) Source of the figures.

Now you have collected some data, you should be able to draw some conclusions.

Unless you are (or will be) the lowest cost producer (supplier), then if selling for the lowest price is your strategy in the medium-term, it could lead to your being driven out of business.

Always look at both side's perception of price. What is significant to you may be irrelevant to your customer.

Consultant thinking: 'Shall I reduce my charge from £500 to £400 per day?'

Meanwhile, client thinking: 'Ten days at £500, for a probable saving of £30,000 – that's a good deal.'

OR:

Salesman: 'I will cut the price of XYSs from £6 to £5 each because of the size of your order.'

Purchaser: 'But can I have 8000 units next week?'

Salesman: 'Oh yes, no problem, we always carry large stocks.'

OR:

Purchaser: 'I have obtained a reduction of 50% on XYZs' components against budget.'

Project Manager: 'So what? They don't make up 1/100,000 of cost. Just make sure we have them in plenty of time: there are penalty clauses.'

In a badly run company, some of the items that have been sitting in stock for years could suddenly become very valuable.

In a nationalised industry there was no ultimate profit responsibility – the Government and the tax payer funded the losses. The industry was production-orientated and, employing serious craftsmen, always produced highly engineered work which was several times better in specification than required. When it went to tender for outside work, the company:

(a)   Costed the work on the basis of its own technical and craft standards – not on the client's requirements. Thus it was usually the highest bidder and obtained very little of the third party work for which it bid.

163

(b)   'Improved' the tolerances and so went over budget whenever a contract was secured.

(c)   (Worst of all) Continued to concentrate on price and ignored its strongest selling point – the quality of its work.

If you are in a production or technically driven company, the engineers will say: 'There is a lot to be said for having products with better specifications and tolerances.' Is that what your customers want? AND do they know they are getting it? How do they know?

How often do you see a company trying to sell on price and at the same time carrying out expensive in-house manufacturing, when what the market is buying are the design skills of two or three people. In this sort of company, look out for such attitudes as:

- 'We should make it here and not import it.'

- 'It is morally wrong.'

- 'What else can we produce in the factories?'

- Or worst of the lot: 'But the equipment is not fully depreciated.'

Take an industry like Airfreight or Parcels, where all the rates may be very similar. Why are people buying from you? I saw several possible reasons:

(a)   A salesman actually went to see the customer and listened to him. No difference in the eventual service or price.

(b)   The van driver in South Wales was very committed. Before van radios or telephones were common, he would visit, extra to his route, certain large customers

164

for whom he did not have a pick-up booked for that day. He would also cold call at some small ones. He added two hours to his working day, for which he received no extra pay and little praise.

(c) The customer's export department was inefficient. Staff made mistakes on routing documentation, and were generally slow-witted. Clerks at the other airfreight divisions were rude to them: they were making them extra work. One clerk in our department would automatically correct everything for them and never draw attention to it. Thirty percent of that office's freight eventually came from that one customer. The customer's staff members were not bothered about getting the best price: they wanted to keep their jobs and feel good.

(d) The manager was effective: cheerful hardworking, and leading his people from the front.

For some reason the company opened an office in Dartford, Kent. This was the smallest industrial catchment area in which it had an office; it was also the smallest premises. The Dartford Manager, however, was very keen, and even expanded his catchment area beyond the Dartford Tunnel and into Essex. Eventually, this office became the company's third largest for export freight in the U.K. Imagine that company's potential if it had found or developed thirty more such men or women.

Consider the highly competitive office furniture and equipment supply business.

A young salesman called cold and subsequently called regularly. He was always polite but rarely secured an order. Then, when the company was moving to a brand new office development, the managing and other directors were far too busy to organise the move, so put the office manageress in charge. This woman had a son of the same age the salesman and she bought all the new furniture and equipment through him. He achieved 50% of his annual target on that one order. It cost his customer no more to buy the furniture than it would have paid other companies. Why did she buy from him? He reminded her of her son and he was always polite.

What is/are your company's unique selling proposition/s? Does it even have one? Look at the managing director of Avis Car Hire. The market research stated that Avis was only the number two in the U.S. car hire industry. That was all that research came up with. Did he despair? No, he made use of the information with a 'We try harder' slogan and the rest is history.

Let's take a man who is going to fly on the Athens to London run. Which airline does he choose?

First Trip: His new secretary books him tourist class on Lufthansa with a plane change at Frankfurt.

Second Trip: As he is senior staff, he flies British Airways, club class. This is his own choice.

Third Trip: Time is short. He has to be at a particular meeting. He flies Swiss Air. It is the only flight that fits the desired times.

Fourth Trip: He is going on holiday, paying his own ticket. XYZ airline – cheapest available ticket on a scheduled flight.

Fifth Trip: His wife is going on holiday with the baby. She flies Olympic as they are fantastic with babies.

So, whilst the same customer is buying the same flight it is his requirements that change each time. If you are in the airline business, rather than the service business, you will miss this point.

People do buy reputation, for example: 'Founded in 1826', 'Queen's Award to Industry', etc. Sometimes they buy by reputation, i.e. what may well be the best product, but which definitely won't lead to criticism for their buying decision: nobody ever got fired for buying an IBM computer system!

What have we not yet done? Have we asked our customers why they are buying from us or other companies? Or, more revealing, why ex-customers stopped buying and what will make them consider buying again? Why have other people never bought from us?

Be careful when you are asking these questions; many customers are too polite to tell you the brutal facts and these are what you really want to hear. Also, remember that your selling points in one country or market are not always the same, or even similar in another market. For instance:

(a) In the U.S., certain types of clothing, fast-food etc., are normal, everyday products. In a third world capital city on the other hand, they may be considered the height of trendiness.

(b) In France, many bistros concentrate on the quality of food, but not the surroundings. The menu is written in French because that is their language. In the heart of English Surrey, however, a large numbers of restaurants with a very high standard of decor, also produce their menus in French. This is to indicate a similarly high quality of food – and the subsequent status attached.

So, I say again, what are you really selling, and what could you be selling?

B

Managing the gross margin

What's this, more accounting jargon? No, it's really an extension of the old saying 'If you watch the pennies, the pounds will look after themselves', or 'Watch the cents and pfennigs and the dollars and marks will look after themselves'.

Let's take a small shop, say a grocers. Here are some annual figures:

	1982	1983	1984	1985	1986
Sales	50,000	60,000	50,000	80,000	90,000
Net profit	5,000	8,000	8,000	9,000	10,000

What does this tell you? – Steady sales growth, apart from a set-back in 1984? Let's look at some more detail:

	1982	1983	1984	1985	1986
Gross Margin	20,000	25,000	23,000	30,000	33,000
As % of Sales	40%	41.6%	46%	37.5%	36.6%

So, the highest gross margin was achieved in a year of sales down-turn: 1984. The gross margin is actually lower now than before.

Let's look now at net profit, percentage and certain overheads:

	1982	1983	1984	1985	1986
NET PROFIT:					
1) As a % of sales revenue	10%	13.3%	16%	11.25%	11%
2) As % of gross margin	25%	32%	35%	30%	30.3%

	1982	1983	1984	1985	1986
OVERHEADS:					
(a) Rent	5,000	5,000	10,000	10,000	10,000
(b) Motor exps	2,000	4,000	500	4,000	6,000
(c) Salaries	4,000	4,000	2,800	10,000	12,000
(d) Seminars	10	30	nil	1,000	3,000

Some explanations:

(a) The shop moved to larger premises in 1984.

(b) In the same year a staff member left, leading to shorter opening hours and hence lower sales.

(c) More staff were recruited in 1985, which led to longer opening hours and higher turnover. The shop owner in theory has a minimum required net profit, i.e. to live on. When times are good, he can afford to:

• run an expensive car for himself and his wife

• and spend money on business improvement seminars at top hotels overseas. This is partially why the gross margin is slipping. He is not actively managing his business: he is not present on his premises much of the time.

This leads to a major truism:

You can only spend on overheads what you generate in gross margin. If not . . . Hello, Mr Liquidator.

Gross margin can be defined as the selling price (net of quantity discounts and sales commissions) less the actual cost of the product (materials, direct labour, distribution cost, and allocation of all costs incurred in producing the product and getting it to the customer).

What margins are your competitors getting? How can you

improve the margin on each product? Can you take extra business at a lower margin to increase the total gross profit? (see the chapter 20 on contribution accounting).

In some businesses, particularly retailing, the gross margin is actively managed. It is not always correctly managed! A retailer may tell me that he wants a 30% margin. BUT, let's look at the following:

Product (A) 1% margin, stockturn 1 week, Annual margin 52%

(B) 30% margin, stockturn 5 weeks, Annual margin 150%

(C) 100% margin, stockturn 1 year, Annual margin 100%

So you say 'fine'. It is the relationship between gross margin and stockturn. Now consider the following – You are selling product (A) only because you are open at convenient times, i.e. when nobody else is. People will buy bulk bags of disposable razors from supermarkets and individual ones from you (when they have run out).

If you increase the price of product (A) from 20p to 25p, your gross margin is increased from a fraction of a penny to 5.02p, i.e. to +25% (of sales value). You will still only be supplying extra razors to people who have run out, but you will make a decent profit from doing it. There is no way you can match the supermarket price, nor should you be trying to do so.

The amount of space an item takes up is also relevant. It may well be that you stock items with low gross margins, but which take up little space. This may give your business a greater overall profit than through stocking fewer high margin and turnover items, but which take up a large amount of space.

So now you know what to do? Good.

Now, what if a supplier offers you credit for a period in excess of the time it takes you to sell the product? In other words, a return on capital which is truly infinity – DECISIONS! DECISIONS!

So what this chapter is saying is:

- Know your margin
- Manage your margin
- Above all, think about your margin on each product.

CHAPTER FIFTEEN

Work in progress – is it work? is it progress?

'I want the profit of this business to be £25,000 in the books this month – how you get to it is your problem.'

If somebody is 'fixing' a set of books to arrive at a pre-determined profit figure, he or she will often adjust the stock figure. However, work in progress is the most popular area to choose. It is a hard area to check for accuracy, and the figures are often vague.

I have seen many types of 'work in progress':

- General engineering components in semi-finished state.
- Drawings and designs for engineering projects.
- Partially-built buildings and support facilities.
- One-off manufacturing projects partially completed
- Partially written computer software.

Each of the above was for a specific order. There is also something called 'speculative' work in progress, where the work is believed to be saleable, possibly to a specific customer on completion.

So what is the work carried out at your company worth to date? Eventually, it will be worth what somebody will pay for it. What is it worth now? That is a difficult question.

The most pathetic method of valuing work in progress is one much-loved by an auditor I once knew: the method of percentage of completion. This involved:

(a) Taking costs to date on the project.

(b) Dividing the result of (a) by the total budgeted costs.

(c) Calculating the cost to date as a proportion on total budgeted costs.

(d) then, actually book profit on long-term unfinished projects, utilising this percentage, for example:

budgeted profit £1,000   total budgeted cost £50,000

cost to date   £25,000   they take $\frac{25,000}{50,000}$ i.e. £500 to profit

Records are often poorly detailed or incomplete, especially with regard to managerial labour! The person making the calculations will always say, 'We are within budget.' Management, being optimistic as usual, will confirm the project will be completed within budget. How often have we heard that!

A good method of valuing work in progress is to have:

(a) A breakdown of original costs.
(b) Units of each material.
(c) Labour – hours by grade.
(d) Any other measurable units.

At an accounting period end, you can then calculate the units of each type still required to complete the contract. Have them valued and the result is the cost to completion and the answer to the present value of your work in progress. BUT there may be work missed, or costs from the original forecast which have not yet been discovered.

You need as accurate a breakdown of cost as possible for each project. Cost control using networks in a simplified form has great potential. With the help of a gifted quantity surveyor, I once managed to manually get a valuation on a building project set up which was very effective for the short time it was in operation. Only one of the five site managers co-operated. After we produced two months figures, he was fired. His replacement and the other four managers from then on just refused to take part.

Now consider the situation in manufacturing industry. Ideally the fashionable 'Just in Time' Kanban systems limit your work in progress, particularly in an assembly business. Materials Requirements Planning is in many ways the application of common sense to planning. As your company is in trouble, there has probably been very little application of common sense before now, particularly in the planning of work. Worse still, your company may have booked partial profits on unfinished work or already received progress payments. So you cannot just stop the work, you have to complete it.

If there are no budgets for Jobs in Progress, have one drawn up. You are not interested in the past, but need to know the units and costs to completion. Once you have these figures, make your production people draw up a network and have the budget put in to this. Just thinking about the sequence of actions in a production process will have a fantastic effect on improving and freeing peoples' attitudes and understanding.

In a manufacturing company, several people can usually estimate or check the times, materials, costs to completion etc. In a computer software company there is probably only one person will be able to estimate the time to completion of a program – the person carrying it out. One of the worst problems in software companies is the lack of documentation of systems which have been developed, and also of programs and amendments to programs.

If you can just stop a project which is going well over budget, it may be worth doing. However it may ruin your credibility with a present client.

IF YOU GO BUST YOU WON'T HAVE ANY CLIENTS!

Can you re-negotiate the agreed price, delivery time etc? Has the client requested any additional modifications since signing the order? Are they documented? It is possible that under the terms of your original project contract, you can receive extra payments in certain circumstances, for instance, industry annual percentage increase for inflation.

Never accept any global figure for work in progress. First, at least have it broken down by project. Then have the starting dates entered, followed by the cost to completion. For large projects, have these drawn into the network, with milestones and actual costs, amounts and dates, if available. IF THERE ARE NONE – GET THEM!

One important advantage of comparing historical actuals with budgeted cost quantities is the opportunity to assess how inaccurate the estimations were. You can then apply these errors to their cost of completion calculations.

A simple job costing system needs to be applied as fast as possible. Keep it simple. It is surprising on the initial analysis just how many costs you will find going into the overheads which are actually specific to a job. With standard component sub-assemblies, obtain rough figures for actual batch costs. This will allow you to compare these with either the actual or theoretical standard cost sheet.

Measurement

Who has measured work achieved to date? Is it accurate? Often in the construction businesses, the amount recorded will be less than the actual work completed, for example:

(a) Count houses completely plastered, not those only partially plastered, even if 90% finished.

(b) Count the floors of a building completed, not the number partially built.

176

Another question that needs to be answered with regard to a new computer program or mechanical device, is, will part or all of if work? Can you test it? If it does not work, a great deal of re-work will be required – which usually isn't budgeted for.

> In a tool making company manufacturing mainly for group companies where 30% of cost was on non-budgeted re-work, a new chartered engineer working on the shop floor had this figure down to 3% within six months. In addition, he was by this time more than covering it in his competitive prices.

In a manufacturing environment, you need to keep work in progress to a minimum, but there has to be the application of common sense. Lead time on supplies is crucial. For instance, you have these units in stock, don't require them machined for two weeks, but your labour force has spare capacity this week. For the next month, it is at full capacity. While the effect of machining these units now will, on paper, increase the work in progress, in practice you will still be paying staff if you don't do it this week. By doing it now, your actual labour opportunity cost is nil on this work.

Also bear in mind technological change. If the project in progress will not be completed until well into the future, it might be surpassed by new technology. Your client may well not want it then. In the world of electronics, this technological obsolescence could occur within a few months. If you are in a turnround situation, the company probably has been very slack with deadlines up to now, and has a history of not meeting deadlines and/or poor records. This could be a valid legal reason for your client not to pay all or part of the money still due. He may even try to get some progress payments returned! He will also have a right to damages!

Some work in progress may be a liability in progress – SO BE CAREFUL!

CHAPTER SIXTEEN

Common sense – how common is it?

Why a chapter on the obvious, you say? Because common sense is not common. Often in the senior and middle-management of firms with serious problems, you will find that it is seriously lacking, or even non-existent.

Many times I have been talking to a clerk or a labourer of 10+ years experience, who says 'I can never understand why they did X. It doesn't make sense – Still, they're the bosses, THEY MUST KNOW WHAT THEY'RE DOING'. The truth is – they often DON'T.

Another group lacking in common sense are the self-confessed business experts who:

- never worked in a commercial business

- never had a real line position

- never had their own money or future at risk

- never set up a business and struggled with it.

Typical members of this group may include:

- audit trained accountants

- bank managers

- high flying M.B.A.'s, straight from university to business school

- solicitors not specialising in commercial work

- retirees, particularly middle-managers from multi-national companies, now acting as business advisors

- management consultants with less than four years experience of actually working in a company.

You will always find:

- ninety-nine out of 100 people who can tell you what is wrong with a business – 99%

- fifty out of 100 people can tell you what needs to be done – 50%

- one in 100 can come up with an action plan – 1%

- one in 10,000 can actually put it into practice – 0.01% right.

People will look to their own interest and survival in the short-term, so you will have to allow for this. There is usually everything to gain by being unorthodox, so long as what you do makes sense. Note, I am saying does it make sense to YOU? Not, is it what everybody else does.

Another thing you should be aware of is that the more years of formal education a person has had, the less streetwise he usually is. In a turnround situation, you have got to get everybody pulling together, NOW. How often do you read an article in a newspaper in which some major sociological study comes up with the obvious? – Obvious to the man in the street, but not the 'Ivory Tower' researcher. For instance, that:

- Ugly women are less attractive to men.

- Fat, bald men are less attractive to women.

- Violent criminals are unhappy people.

- People who live in the worst housing have the lowest incomes.

How many man hours and how much money have gone into these 'research' projects?

1) An Engineer Promoted Off Site And Into The Office

   (a) Suddenly everything has to be typed.

   (b) Filing abounds.

Efficient Manager's In Tray

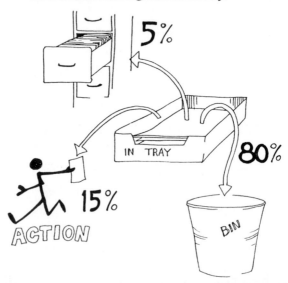

   (c) He plays the executive role model. Who does it impress? Well, it impresses the media (looking for stereotypes) and other people acting out similar executive roles. Your real down-to-earth business-man or woman will only see through it to overheads and inefficiency.

In Saudi Arabia a managing director, newly promoted from his engineering job, started turning up to work every day wearing a three-piece suit – despite the fact that it was the height of summer (35 degrees centigrade) and the premises were awful. The other workers, impressed by the look of this, started to follow his 'example'. What nobody realised was that this man just did not sweat. He was comfortable – his staff were not. Most competitors came to the conclusion that they were either crazy or posers, or both. In other words, the smart clothes did nothing to improve the quality of the company's work, nor its profitability.

(d) Secretarial and clerical staff have their work routines thrown into chaos – simply because high flyers didn't want to be seen to – or can't be bothered to – to dial their own calls.

2) Out Of The Factory – Into The Sales Office

(a) All production-orientated people 'know' that sales staff are an overhead; and why the sales department cannot sell all the wonderful products that production produce, the advantages of which are obvious to the production people, God knows! Salespeople, on the other hand, keep asking for changes to standard models and delivery dates which means small production runs and ruins production efficiency (note – not profitability) and economic batch quantities.

(b) Non-salespeople look at the travel expenses, the meals etc. 'Why, he only saw two clients. There was no sale arising from either of them! (ignoring future possibilities). 'There is an enormous amount of waste.' Non, or occasional business travellers don't realise that regular travel can be very tiring and boring.

Keep asking: 'Am I missing the obvious?' Sometimes it is useful to have someone as a sounding board. That is the role of a good consultant.

Common sense

Common sense dictates that time is precious – don't spend hours in formal meetings. Hold informal ones to spread information – and not just with senior staff. Enforce a time limit on meetings. Have an agenda. If you are not an effective chairman yourself, nominate somebody, or better still, move the job around different staff members. Hold meetings at the start or at the end of the day – not in precious commercial time. Restrict the numbers of figures mentioned at meetings and in reports to significant ones only. Encourage everybody. Keep it simple. Keep it short.

Common sense also states that in a turnround situation, you have got to quickly build confidence in your own staff, customers, suppliers, bankers and investors. If you are not confident in yourself, in your abilities and that you can turn your business round, then don't take on the role. Note, the word was confident, not arrogant. Don't take the attitude:

- Everything was wrong here until I came.

- Another mess to sort out.

- Our company taking yours over has saved your jobs.

It is vital to be truthful with your employees and let them know what you can, as soon as you can. This will build respect, if not affection. The latter will probably only appear after the crisis is over, by which time you may have already left for a fresh challenge.

CHAPTER SEVENTEEN

Timesheet – the organisation

Most cost accounting in industry originated at a time when 99% plus of employees were either production operatives or factory workers, and was based on work studies. When incentive systems were employed, they were usually based on piece work, so it was necessary to record peoples names against the quantities produced. As engineering and clothing companies developed, plans for future production schedules, machine loading etc., were based on these records.

In a vehicle manufacturers producing relatively few standard vehicles, but with any number of possible equipment options, employee breakdown totalled 500 staff workers and 2,500 factory workers. Of the factory employees, 500 were carrying out non-recordable work: foreman, shop clerks, security, material handling, labourers etc. The rest of the factory staff worked piece rate. The staff were just counted as an overhead, supposedly controlled by budget. In other words, whole departments of draftsmen and clerical staff existed which had no system of costing time to products. Once staff were on the payroll, nobody measured their output. Departments grew by X% each year. None were ever reduced in size or closed. The company also had a bonus system: some months a bonus was paid and in others, nothing. The bonus was based on the number of vehicles despatched. So if a member of staff had to work overtime on, say, an investment grant return, he might receive an extra premium of 3%, 5% 10% or nil.

Not surprisingly, after a couple of years of this situation, the company went bust. The product was nevertheless a worthwhile one, and a slimmed down company now exists as a subsidiary of another, in which everybody knows what he or she is doing!

Most professional firms: architects, engineers, management consultants, lawyers, auditors, etc., employ a system of staff timesheeting. In most cases its main purpose is to see that the work gets billed. Sheets are filled in at the end of a period, be it a week or a month, usually on an estimated basis, from a diary that exists for this purpose and for the purpose of claiming expenses.

So, the use of a timesheet is staff control? – WRONG!

This is but one purpose. In professional firms, most of the engineers, lawyers, accountants, etc., are production workers and their time-sheets form the basis of the costing. You will therefore need to timesheet everybody – starting first of all with you. If the person at the top of an organisation does not complete one regularly, then it will become a status symbol to follow suit: 'I am also a senior staff member, and too important to complete a timesheet.'

In a professional organisation you can:

(a) Build up a data base of the time to perform certain tasks.

(b) Use this for pricing future work and budgetary control on present jobs.

(c) Look at how you can improve your productivity.

(d) Circulate your chargeable time and cost rates.

After three years of building up the records of draftsmen's time in one company, we had a very useful data base. The managing director read an article revealing that the ratio of engineers to draftsmen was 0.25 : 1 in the U.S.A. Our own ratio was 1 : 1.25. This cost analysis therefore justified our buying and introducing a computer aided drawing system. Previously, much of the draughtsmen's time was spent re-doing a whole drawing, just to add a couple of drains or for a slip road to be slightly re-designed or sited. What used to take two days now took ten minutes.

(e) Take a record of holidays and sickness which can prove invaluable. Surprising how few companies keep accurate, signed records.

(f) Start to investigate intangibles.

A category existed: 'Professional Development'. What did it mean? We broke it down into:

- Specified planned training.
- Specified external courses.
- Idle – but using time constructively.

This led to the identification of spare capacity which, by using contribution techniques, could be sold profitably. It also meant a better sharing of staff between departments. A priority list was then developed which identified required in-house studies projects. Thereafter, when somebody had time available, they could be allocated a suitably useful task.

Another fascinating category was 'Practice Development'. After introducing a few codes, we were quickly able to identiy whether this was geographic development or product development areas. We were also looking to see whether it was planned or ad hoc (i.e. utilisation of idle time). By allocating different developments a specific job number, it was possible to estimate when a specific project would come to an end. We could then assess the results which in turn could be used for planning future development work.

(g) Put an overhead recovery system into operation.

(h) Assist staff in time control and planning.

185

Do make use of timesheets: they are a cheap and simple way of revealing and obtaining vital information that could save you thousands of pounds in the future, and the system only costs a few minutes of a person's time every day. Their major advantage in the turnround situation is to find out what everybody thinks he or she is doing. Systems based on hours are most effective; though occasionally, you may find half hours is more appropriate. There should be an average of six entries a day per person, although the number could be as high as twenty, or as low as one.

Let's look at a member of staff usually classed under the category of overheads. What can the timesheet reveal in this situation?

1)   What does the secretary record?

- 4 hours – Typing.

- 1 hour – Making calls.

- 1 hour – Taking shorthand.

- 1 hour – Opening/distributing post.

- 1 hour – Purchasing.

Well it's a useful start. Next, what exactly was the typing, and for whom?

- 1 hour – Typing invoices.

- 2 hours – Typing memos and related shorthand.

- 1 hour – Typing sales proposals.

2)   Now let's have a look at the finance director:

- 2 hours – Reviewing Press. (i.e. reading Financial Times)

Tell him to read it at home.

- 3 hours – Cash Flow work on personal computer. (Playing with computer – should read Chapter Nine)

- 1 hour – Attending management meetings.

- 1 hour – Dictating letters. (Did he have to dictate them? Are there no standard letters in use? Also, if the letters were drafted instead, he could have saved the secretary's time. Couldn't some of these letters have been handwritten, or phone calls made instead?)

- 1 hour – Lunch with Bank Manager. (Probably more like two hours.) Was the company paying? Does the company expect any advantage? What? If it is not quantifiable, this is socialising – not work!

- 1.5 hours – Meeting with auditors. (Does this man know we are in trouble? Was a meeting necessary? Did it need to take so long?)

- 1 hour – Completion of study on delivery costs.

- 2 hours – Writing and signing salary cheques. (We don't need salaries to be secret. Highly paid staff should be able to justify their salary to their peers. So somebody is getting high sales commissions or performance bonus. Let's shout it from the rooftops. Can't somebody else write the cheques for the financial director to check and sign them? Why not use bank transfer?)

- = 12.5 hours in total – BUT AROUND TWO/THREE PRODUCTIVE HOURS!

Clerical departments

Start to measure, for example:

- How many letters received?
- How many invoices checked?
- How many cold telephone sales calls?
- How many coupons received?
- How many letters sent out?
- How many orders placed?
- How many samples tested?
- How many support calls taken/solved?
- How many mechanic call outs?

Formulate a list along these lines. If you want to succeed, initially you should state that there will be no staff reductions (and mean it). You are just re-deploying people for more useful tasks.

You need a simple but flexible coding system. You should also read through the sheets quickly once a week. You will learn a lot. My preferred method is to use a detailed coding system at first. You will then be able to get a good feel as to whom is doing what. Rationalise it afterwards.

As my accounting lecturer at Derby used to say years ago: 'And remember the cost of costing.'

Everybody is paid to come to work. You need to utilise people effectively. A timesheet is of value both to the individual and to the company. It is an opportunity to make and to save money.

CHAPTER EIGHTEEN

Distribution – the Cinderella area

There is only time to touch on some aspects of distribution. How significant this cost is depends largely on the type of company you are trying to turn round. Often distribution costs, if separately analysed by product, can amount to a significant proportion of the total product cost. Remember, the same principal probably applies to the costs of your inbound supplies.

Distribution costs are usually high for goods which are:

- bulky in relation to their weight, for instance, foam rubber, glass bottles, etc.

- perishable, for instance, cut flowers.

- easily disposed of by thieves, for instance, cigarettes, spirits etc.

Example of a product with high distribution costs:

- A case of wine costs you £10.

- The Government will add an excise duty of £10.

- The cost to the shopkeeper is £30 plus V.A.T.

- This gives you a contribution to controllable cost and profit of £10.

- It costs you £1 per case in freight cost from your supplier to your warehouse, and £3 per case delivery from the warehouse to the shopkeeper with a minimum shipment size of three cases, i.e. minimum delivery charge of £9.

- The minimum you can deliver is:

	2 Cases	3 Cases
Revenue	60	90
Wine and Duty	40	60
Freight	2	3
Delivery	<u>9</u>	<u>9</u>
Contribution	9	18

In other words, an increase of 50% in the size of your minimum drop, increases your contribution by 100%.

If you could reduce your delivery cost to £2:

	1 Case	2 Cases	3 Cases
Revenue	30	60	90
Wine and Duty	20	40	60
Freight	1	2	3
Delivery	<u>6</u>	<u>6</u>	<u>6</u>
Contribution	3	12	31

So, a 33% reduction in your delivery cost has enabled you both to service smaller customers, and has increased the contribution on:

- 2 case delivery by 33.3%, and on
- 3 case delivery by 72%.

Allocate direct costs of distribution

There are two ways to do this – by customer or by product. The former can make a transaction profitable which the latter has initially shown to be unprofitable.

Remember that you are not just allocating bought-in

transport and warehousing, but all costs specifically incurred by you, including handling, packing, warehousing and the very high costs of forwarding. The latter is even higher when exporting, as it involves special paperwork.

> When I first started commercial accountancy training, I was sent to spend a week at a a railway goods yard. The railways had a rate for general freight. Members of the management were very proud as they had just secured an export consignment, a sawing machine for France. They had not gone out and sold this service; indeed, the customer had found them. A wagon spent two weeks in the yard idle, and a specially erected cover was placed over it. Two men spent the best part of these two weeks carefully packing the machine. The company, however, would have charged the same price to somebody who had turned up with four packing cases and had them loaded in five minutes to the same destination. Figures:

	£
Revenue	<u>125</u>
Freight Charge	100
Cost of two men for two weeks	200
Cost of idle wagon	?
Cost of wagon cover	?

> So they had lost money before they moved it.

Using third parties

Why not? The reason for the growth of so many parcels and distribution companies is that they do a good job (more often than not) compared with in-house transport, and obtain better asset utilisation. To some degree, the people who are best at particular service functions should go and work for themselves. Be careful. Make sure you are not paying for services which you don't require.

Some people would pay for an air freight company to get goods to another location in the U.K. the next day. However, to consolidate freight, many air freight companies used to use trucks on short distances, for example, Manchester to London. Thus, a national air freight shipment might never see a plane. In such cases, an overnight parcels service would have been cheaper and probably quicker.

Export

If you do not export very often, use a professional forwarder until you at least know what is involved.

The first point of call for information is either a Chamber of Commerce or a good commercial library: Manchester, Birmingham, City Business Library in London, etc.

If you don't get the paperwork correct, it can be a disaster:

(a) Goods get stuck in the docks.

(b) I have heard of customs warehouses in Africa full of imported machinery and goods on which importers cannot afford do pay the duty. Hence, they cannot get and use the machinery to produce goods to export, which would in turn pay for the machinery. A truly vicious circle.

(c) Goods sent air freight with a collection of freight and goods value at destination. Great for a local agent – he would collect, but exchange control in some countries would not let him remit.

(d) The wrong customs duty tariff is applied due to the description of the goods being wrongly entered on a customs form. This leads to extra unanticipated unrecoverable costs.

Equally, in some countries local staff can produce minor miracles via paperwork. I remember a man in Asia once who managed to import and export a car which never physically came into the country. BUT, I also remember going to clear some household goods in Greece. Speaking virtually none of the language, I found the system very complicated. I was sent from person to person, for what reasons I did not understand. The staff could not have been more helpful. Other people who used agents took all day, whilst I had finished in three hours.

Your own transport fleet (not cars)

In many companies, depending on the type of vehicle owned (or used) they could be used for both collecting supplies and delivering goods. You need to collect sufficient statistics – mileage, fixed costs, variable costs – to cost vehicles. The results of the analysis can be very revealing.

> Working for a drilling company in the Middle East, I analysed the costs of vehicles and then examined them by the job title of the allocated driver, also the rig to which they were allocated.
>
> Of the six categories of driver, it was clear which had by far the highest costs – mechanics, in fact an average of 30% more. When analysed by rig, out of nine rigs, some had high costs for all categories of drivers, others were always low. So, it was discovered that vehicle running costs were effected by management, and significant savings started to be made immediately.

Log sheets for the journey are vital:

(a) To ensure costs are allocated.

(b) Much more importantly – to ensure that any chargeable work is not missed.

Even if you only have a couple of runabout vehicles, this can be expensive.

A firm had two production sites just four miles apart, and two vehicles. Sometimes staff would deliver finished products or materials for working on by third parties. Sometimes they would collect supplies or transfer goods between the two sites. These two vehicles were probably the main vehicles used in the town for furniture removals etc., and each could easily run up over 1000 miles per week. The main problem was that it was an engineering company who was running them. The vehicles were not being controlled; again, they were just considered an overhead.

Drivers, particular those with Heavy Goods Vehicle licences, are highly skilled people. They are also expensive. You therefore need to ensure both the maximum of productive time and that the law is followed in relation to hours worked.

Presumably when a vehicle is on the road, the main reason that it is painted in your livery is positive promotion. If all you can afford is a filthy battered van, then your name is better left off! The power of vehicle advertising is quite strong, so it is important to get a good image. For instance, the punchline of a plumber's van regularly seen on the M62 was, Singh & Singh 'You've tried the cowboys – now try the Indians.' Is your firm utilising its vehicles so positively?

Now try the Indians

195

It should also be remembered that having your own transport, even if it is only a van, can add to your flexibility and profit. If I want a product NOW, I will pay extra for it. Some companies will utilise their own staff and hire vehicles out, perhaps even the office manager in his car, if such an opportunity arose. So:

- Do you know why you have your transport fleet or vehicles?

- Do you know what they are doing?

- Do you know what they are costing?

- Do you know what contribution they are making?

Distribution as a profit centre

Do you include distribution in your product costing? Is the amount realistic? Who says it is? What do competitors charge? Are they covering some of the distribution cost from the product price?

	A	B
Product Price	10	10
Plus X		4
	--	--
Price quoted to customer	10	14
Plus delivery cost	6	2
	--	--
	16	16

The eventual price the customer pays is the same. Company A quotes a lower unit price. Who would you buy from? Company A at £10 plus delivery, or Company B at £14 plus delivery? Some people will go for cheapest product and ignore delivery cost. Others will go for the cheapest delivery. Others still will arrange to collect to save delivery cost, or will pay extra for speed. They want it now.

Do you hold stocks for customers at no cost to them? Does this eventually add to your profits? Are you sure? Could the warehouse holding customer goods be put to other use? Would this affect the bottom line?

Are you charging for all special packaging? 'It's included in the price.' Is it? Are you charging for all deliveries?

A company producing patterns for the clothing industry used to drastically undercharge for the quality of its work. That is, pricing was based on the labour cost of work and not the value of that work to the customer. Staff would rush out and deliver by car up to 100 miles each way, the company paying for the petrol and the cost of its staff members' time.

Delivery had not been charged for because 'It costs us nothing'! The company was later amazed to discover that its customers would not only pay for delivery, but also pay a premium.

Alternatively, you will find that some product goes out in the rep's. car or the company van/truck, with no third party extra cost to the supplying company. Why is it not charged? Profit is not a dirty word – neither is fuel free!

People also forget to charge communication costs connected with special jobs: telex, special post, courier, etc. Similarly, many delivery firms seem to base their charging on geographical distance. No allowance is made for the cost of time involved, particularly when there is a strong possibility of traffic delays, diversions etc.

Paperwork

No matter how large or how small your distribution,

whether you do it yourself or not – *get your paperwork right*.

Are you insured?

What for?

Do you have delivery notes?

Are conditions of trade attached?

Have you had them checked?

Do you always insist on getting signatures for deliveries?

Are they legible? Ensure they are not signed 'Fred' in blunt pencil, or 'Donald Duck'. Ensure none are missing.

Is there any excessive vehicle waiting time to charge?

Do you pay insurance for each shipment via third parties, or do you have a global policy?

Do you make claims in time? No? Why not? Yes? Are you sure?

Are you on a special rate? Does the invoice reflect this?

Do you use more than one carrier? This is good practice, as it enourages competition.

Does your distribution system add value?

1) So you sell via wholesalers rather than direct to retailers. It does save transport costs.

2) Does it lead to maximisation of profit? It could be the only way to get economical drops to the shops. Or it could mean your product does not move fast enough and the wholesalers drop it.

3) Does your packaging add to the attractiveness of your product? Is it efficient for stacking?

Cash flow – own versus third party distribution

If cost was the only criteria, and the cost of third parties' service was the same as your own, which would be beneficial from a cash flow?

* Represents time of payment of cost incurred

WEEK	1	2	3	4	5	6	7	8
	—	—	—	—	—	—	—	—
								*
Third Party	nil	nil	nil	nil	nil	nil	nil	Pay Week 1 Freight
Own – Wages	*	*	*	*	*	*	*	*
Vehicle Fixed	*							
Variable	*	*	*	*	*	*	*	*
Warehousing	*	*						

The most beneficial is obvious.

Conclusion

A lot of money is to be made and saved in distribution. Do not ignore it. Let's say you are a small company sending out 100 parcels per week. If you save £1 per parcel – that's £5,000 per year!

CHAPTER NINETEEN

Listen

Let's start with a story from a colonial war. A verbal message is sent:

'Send reinforcements – I'm going to advance.'

By the time this message has been passed verbally from tired to fresh despatch rider, the following message was received at headquarters:

'Send three and fourpence – I'm going to a dance.'

Reinforcements

In addition to listening, this chapter is also about reading reports and actually *reading* what is being said – not pre-judging.

The worst listeners fall into groups:

- The ex-military officer – the self-styled 'good at leading' man. This may be, but he is not used to being talked back at, nor will he listen to what is being said.

- The know-all graduate who will condescendingly listen before dismissing what he is told with a 'Good point, I've taken that into account.'

Remember that your time is in short supply. Whereas everybody at some stage of their life usually comes up with a pearl of wisdom, you need to be careful with your time; otherwise you could spend days listening to voluminous amounts of unoriginal garbage and story-telling.

Junior-in-rank employees with long service, often do not have a great deal to say, but they can offer some unusual and fundamental insights. They are also the people most likely to come up with short-term cost savings or incremental revenue ideas. In many cases, they know a great deal, particularly about personal characteristics of other staff, but don't think what they know is important.

It is useful to be tuned into the office grapevine. Once you know who is friendly with whom, including at competitors' and suppliers' establishments; who socialises with whom; even who is sleeping with whom, then many apparently irrational decisions, comments and actions become clear.

It is important to have an open door, but keep the conversations short. Listen and then ask pertinent questions.

By listening, I don't mean spending time in various consultation meetings which are often very formal. The best information comes from individuals or small groups. Some of the information you gather will not be useful in its own right; it is a framework on which you can hang unconnected information to see something which is. Thus, time spent at the coffee machine or walking around the office is not wasted.

Are you listening for new opportunities?

You are manufacturing a standard product in a package. There has been very little change in this product for years, but sales are buoyant. Amongst the mail is a handwritten piece of torn notepaper on which is written: 'If I can save you a significant amount of cost, will you give me 50% of the savings?' What do you do?

(a) Throw it away, it isn't even typed.

(b) Throw it away. If anybody was going to come up with such a practical idea, your development people would have done – are you not the industry leader?

(c) Send a polite reply, basically saying 'go away'.

(d) Give the person half an hour (and the legal agreement he wants, before you see him). Say 'yes' to his proposal and restrict the interview to 15 - 30 minutes.

The industry in question was a safety match company who went for method (d) and the suggestion? –

'Only put the sandpaper to strike the match on one side, not two sides of the box.'

You may think this is obvious. Most good ideas arise from the position of hindsight. *This one, however, cut 8% off the company's production costs and added 50% to its profits, after paying the commission.*

How

Retail Price	100%
Total Costs	90%
Gross Profit	10%
Sandpaper cost as % of Retail Price	20%
After suggestion it is	15%

Effect of cost saving idea on Gross Profit

Original Gross Profit	10%
Add Net Saving	5%
New Gross Profit	15%

Are you picking these ideas up?

You are trying to survive. To turn the company round. Why care about setting precedents? If things don't improve there will be no company. Once a good idea works and is rewarded, more will follow.

Any special deals (only tax and legal aspects are necessary constraints – i.e. it must be legal) – give an incentive.

Any reports are a mine of information – if people are encouraged to write them.

Other sources of information can be found from and around:

1) Your salesmen who know a great deal about –

   - Competitors.

   - What your customers say they want.

   - What is happening in customers' organisations.

2) Delivery drivers – both your own drivers, third party drivers, and suppliers' drivers.

3) Credit control departments and complaints departments.

4) Wholesalers, retailers and the latters' shop staff.

Good listening does not mean reacting to everything you are told and following it up. It is people knowing that you have listened. Try to explain to them the reasons if or why you have not followed what has been said. This feedback leads to more information forthcoming.

Listening also leads to good employee relations, if properly handled. After all, employees can all participate in the information gathered to suggest tactical and strategic decisions.

Why is it that successful growth companies often have a team of two or three very different individuals running the company? Apart from the obvious synergy of different skills and insights, such teams enable people to have a sounding board or devil's advocate.

Two heads are usually better than one.

CHAPTER TWENTY

Contribution accounting – use it

There is a production line which can produce three products. Overheads are apportioned on the basis of machine hours.

	Product A	Product B	Product C
	======	======	======
Revenue per unit	£6	£10	£3
Cost (Including allocated overhead)	£3	£6	£3.50
Profit	£3	£4	–£0.50

So, if we drop product C we will be better off? – WRONG

Let's look at the direct costs and the volume produced of each product.

	Product A			Product B			Product C		
	======			======			======		
	Units			Units			Units		
Volume	5000	@ £6	£30,000	1000	@ £10	£10,000	100,000	@ £3	£300,000
Direct Cost		@ £2	(10,000)		@ £5	(5,000)		@ £1	(100,000)
Contribution (to overheads and profits			£20,000			£5,000			£200,000

So if the company had stopped making product C, it would have been £200,000 worse off. It is unlikely that the product lines of A and B could carry the extra overheads if product C was not making its significant contribution.

It probably would be impossible in the short/medium-term to cut sufficient overheads for A and B production to cover them. So the company may have ceased to exist.

Pricing

You should price on what the market will bear for the volume you wish to sell. However, you need to cover your present cost. In the short-term, while introducing a new product, until production builds up to a certain planned breakeven volume to cover all costs, a company may be selling at a loss.

Item XX3		Month 1	Month 2	Month 3
	Sales in Units	500	15,000	150,000
	Revenue (£)	1,500	15,000	150,000
£1.50 per unit	Direct Cost	750	7,500	75,000
	Contribution			
	to overheads/profit	750	7,500	75,000
	Less production and			
	other Overheads	15,000	15,000	15,000
	Net Profit (Loss)	14,250	7,500	60,000
		Loss	Loss	Profit

So what is contribution?

It is the sales revenue less the direct costs of manufacturing and supplying that product. From sales revenue will have been deducted volume discounts and sales commissions.

Direct cost will be direct material, i.e. actually included or used to make the product.

Direct labour could be total cost of men divided by productive hours. Other direct costs could include hire of equipment specially for job; packaging and delivery costs, etc.

The contribution is that amount left from sales revenue after meeting the direct costs. It is available to cover overhead costs and the balance is profit.

Example of an organisation:

	Factory 1	Factory 2	Factory 3	Factory 4	Factory 5	Factory 6
Sales	10	12	15	12	12	10
Direct Cost	4	3	1	9	7	4
Contribution	+6	+9	+14	+3	+5	+6
Less factory overhead	4	6	9	2	3	2
Contribution after factory overhead	+2	+3	+5	+1	+2	+4
Total contribution for region		= +10			= +7	
Cost of regional office		-6			-3	
Total contribution available to cover head office over-		+4			+4	
heads and profit			= + 8			
Less head office cost			-7			
PROFIT			+1			

207

Questions:

1) Why does Factory 3 have such a high contribution?

   ANSWER – It is highly mechanised and hence has a high factory overhead, and low direct labour cost.

2) Are rents included, or notional rent (i.e. a theoretical rent for buildings you own)?

   ANSWER – Some factories may be owned, others rented.

3) What is the capacity of the factories? What changes could take place? What is stopping that happening? What resources, especially cash, over what time scale would be required?

OTHER APPROACHES TO OVERHEAD RECOVERY

Absorption costing

All overhead is recovered against production or sales by means of allocation and apportionment (which is often arbitrary and misleading). This can be especially true of electronic products produced in highly automated factories where the direct cost is miniscule and the overhead percentage to be allocated to the product is several hundred or thousand percent of the product direct cost. In these cases, allocation would be based on machine hours.

Opportunities of contribution acounting

1) You don't automatically recover overhead. Therefore you are more likely to look at it and do something about it.

2) It makes your thinking flexible. 'I am a firm of consulting engineers. In my main office I have twenty-six engineers. All time on jobs is pre-planned. In week six I have two engineers free for thirty hours.' You are not going to fire those men because you have no work for them that specific week.

If a normal engineer charge-out rate is £60 per hour, cost is £30, overhead recovery is £20, and profit is £10; what is the lowest you can charge them out for? £30? WRONG. You have nothing for them to do, anything over £1 will go directly to your profits.

You have to be careful, though!

(a) When pricing for similar or repeat work in future, look at the cost and labour utilisation at the time. If staff are now fully utilised, your charge out rate would have to go back up to £60.

(b) How do you explain to your client that this job cost £200 in June and the same job eight weeks later in August is going to cost £6000?

Activity costing

This is what all the finance based management consulting practices are now selling.

It is an attempt to achieve better allocation by collecting costs in pools and allocating on a basis of costs of activities. For large companies it can be a good idea. Anything which looks at the costs of providing each inhouse service and whether products really need that service, is going to be healthy for your business. You personally don't have time for this in the short-term. Nor can you afford major firms of consultants to do it. A good self-employed management accountant should potentially pay for himself several times over doing this work for you.

CONCLUSION

You can find whole books on the subject of contribution accounting. For your purposes, this chapter should provide you with all you need to know.

CHAPTER TWENTY-ONE

Overseas Operations

For overseas operations all which has been said in other chapters is still relevant, but pay special emphasis to the areas highlighted in this chapter. They will not all be applicable to every Country in which you have operations.

Language – verbal

'Yes' was the only word these men knew and they continued to repeat it with pride. Maybe this is an extreme example, but it shows the problems of communications.

- On a construction site in Iran, we had forty plus nationalities on site. One of our men could sit with a room full of people and talk to each in his own language. He was a fantastic linguist who could move quickly from Farsi to German, to French, to Hebrew, to Italian, to English, to Arabic. He was probably also a very competent foreman. As a site manager though, his linguistic skills were a major disadvantage. He never had time to plan the project, nor take an overview on progress. He worked incredibly hard solving short-term problems and became completely bogged down in detail. He was used as an interpreter and had no time for his own job.

- In the late 1960s in the Gulf, there was a fantastic explosion of work, particularly construction projects. Much of the local population could not speak a European language and most of the expatriates from the U.S.A., Europe and Asia could not speak any Arabic. Dual linguists from other parts of the Arab world were therefore in great demand. Sometimes non-engineers would take construction projects and then sub-contract all the work! Few of the linguists were particularly good engineers, architects, accountants, or whatever.

  By the late 1970s the huge amounts of money invested in education by the Gulf States started to pay off. Local nationals had both qualified as engineers and had a good working knowledge of English. For their companies they bought in the skills required. They did not need linquists.

It is important to learn a few phrases of a language and to carry a phrase book/dictionary. Where possible, you should try to conduct business in your own language or the language used in the area, or English.

Some of the worst misunderstandings arise when people supposedly speaking the same language communicate, or try to, especially when its their native tongue, for example, with English. An English Geordie and an American from the Deep South can be a recipe for disaster. Similarly Arabic between an Arab from the Gulf and an Arab from the Magreb countries of Northern Africa.

Language – written

Do not be lulled into a sense of false security just because you have something in writing. The literal interpretation can differ hugely from your understanding of what is said. If you have to make a decision based on financial data written in English by a foreign company have it checked to make sure you both mean the same thing and that nothing has been lost or distorted in the transaction.

Information is more important now than later – even truer over longer distances. Information on a telex or handwritten faxed sheet, is often preferable to formal typed reports sent by mail.

The same information in financial reports, even between two countries using the same language, can be radically different e.g. Stocks (inventory in U.S.A.) are valued at L.I.F.O. (last in first out) in U.S. balance sheets and at the lower of costs F.I.F.O. (first in first out) or market value in U.K. balance sheets.

Location

Why is it that companies successfully based, say, in the U.S. Midwest will open their U.K. office in Central London; whilst U.K. companies based in Warrington or Taunton will have their French subsidiary company based in Paris, their Australian head office in Sydney and their U.S. office in New York or Los Angeles? These business capitals will always be in the highest local cost locations. If they also have a manufacturing plant in that country, it will be located out in the wilds, perhaps Iowa in the U.S.A. or Britany in France, or Teesside in the U.K. Common sense, with regard to location and cost, certainly seem to fly out the window when companies 'go international'.

213

If you take over an international company use the same cost rules as you would in this country.

General background

Many of the booklets put out by certain international accountancy practices are full of useful information on:

- Law – including Labour Law
- Tax
- Financial Reporting

Read any reports you can find on your international operations and the countries in which they operate. Banks will sometimes have a useful general guide booklet.

In the first instance, arrange for the local national general manager to come and see you. You are too busy to waste your time going to Paris or Rome or Bombay, whilst a visit to Widnes or wherever will be very enlightening for him. Listen carefully to what he has to say and if necessary get an interpreter. If the information you want is not available from him, and the controls you require are not in operation, give written instructions to have it done and in what time scale, having first discussed it.

Depending on the size of the operation, arrange independent visits quite soon afterwards by the sales and financial directors. Also, if you have a significant manufacturing subsidiary, don't forget the production director.

How many times does the opposite happen?

On a week's trip to France, part of a trip to several European countries, I was assigned to check operating controls. I did not speak French. When I next saw the managing director he said, 'How on earth did you go on in our Paris office – apart from the manager, nobody can speak English.' The M.D. always spoke in French (badly) when he visited that office. However, the whole office spoke English. Even the van driver spoke some – but none of them liked to upset the M.D. by showing him up. I came back from this one trip knowing more about the Paris office staff as individuals than the M.D. had in thirty trips.

Special problems

1) Exchange Control

   It is no use your local subsidiary companies making good profits if you cannot remit them at some stage. Nor is there any sense making offshore payments to people working in a country if you cannot remit funds from that country to cover these costs.

   Based on the international branch accounts showing the amounts of money remitted in U.S. dollars and the additional payments made outside the company an operation in an African country was making losses. In fact, in local currency the company was very profitable, but the expatriate senior manager was only interested in what went into his pocket. He did not even bother to get his paperwork right so that the allowed proportion of monies on projects could be legally transferred.

   It is not viable to sell the company if you cannot remit the proceeds. Of such a sale, which is better?

   (a) A depreciating non-transferable currency?

   (b) Or productive assets and a company paying its way in local currency?

2) Withholding Taxes

   You pay monies as tax on certain payments which are

made overseas, irrespective of whether or not they are payments for costs incurred. They might include interest, professional services, etc. Items and rates vary from country to country.

3) Dividends

You may pay tax at a very high rate on these, or in other countries you may find that the authorities encourage you to take them. As long as there are no other problems take your dividends. Try to organise your affairs to make the most of your profits in countries where taxation is reasonable or low. A sensible company should expect to pay some corporation tax in all countries where operations are successful.

4) Local Shareholding

Local shareholders may be interested in profits and future growth. The parent company may be interested mainly in remittances. You are interested in the turnround situation, i.e. cash flow. (There may be rules about divesting a certain proportion of share capital to local shareholders, for example, the Malaysian Bumi Putra rules.)

Irrespective of what agreements you have or what your consolidated accounts say, the assets in a country are owned by the local company/branch. If a local shareholder has a majority of the shares he controls ALL those assets, not you.

5) Labour Law

Certain countries have very strict systems whereby employers must pay indemnities to workers who have reached the end of their service; usually these are based on final salary and benefits. Expatriate general managers come and go. They often increase salaries and benefits without understanding the long-term repercussions on liabilities.

- A draughtsman had 19 years service in Saudi Arabia when he left. Most draughtsmen stayed only two, and a maximum of four years.

  This man achieved, due to his long service, both a salary and position higher than one would have expected of someone with his qualifications.

Monthly salary Engineer	£1,100	to	£2,000
Draughtsman	£300	to	£600
Special Draughtsman	£1,800		

  During his last two years of service his salary doubled. The generous labour law in the Kingdom was based on X number of months per years service at <u>Final Salary</u>. His leaving benefit was over £100,000.

  Good luck to the man. It was the general manager's lack of understanding of the total cost of his short-term actions which cost the comapny dearly.

- A multinational operating a branch in Greece had new expatriate General Managers approx every two years. Unable to read Greek they quite happily signed documents produced by certain members of the staff. By the time somebody did a salary comparison they were paying secretaries ten times the market rate.

Legal problems

In some countries, corruption is a fact of commercial life. It may not even be seen as corruption; often it is part of the local culture. You cannot judge people living in their own country by other people's standards and culture.

In some countries fraud is rampant. Who actually knows what exactly has been paid? You can put money on it that the main culprits when you want to remove them (due to their incompetence), have in their possession all sorts of incriminating documents.

> Working abroad, I discovered that, with the right paperwork, it was possible to legally transfer money out of the country when a project was complete. The general manager was under pressure. He was costing a fortune in foreign currency and had remitted nothing due to his idleness. Just before a visiting financial executive arrived, the general manager managed to smuggle out about 300,000 U.S. dollars, of which 200,000 arrived in the international company's account. Almost certainly he had pocketed a significant part of $100,000. The local company could not close its annual financial accounts and have them audited as it had a massive shortage of funds which could not be explained. Thus, the company could not get the certificate required to transfer several hundred thousand dollars to the home company. The money was in the bank in local currency but the situation was – no audited accounts – no tax payment certificate – no transfer of funds certificate.

Some companies actually prosper by being honest in corrupt markets. IBM has always stated that it would not pay bribes, and made this a well known fact. So, a corrupt official would always actively consider buying from IBM. Why? – It was known to be a straight company, so if the official bought from IBM, he must in turn be honest – and people would consequently disregard his other purchases, on which he was taking money.

Markets

Some of your overseas operations may have dominant market positions in the local market. They may be much more profitable than the parent company. They may need investment – which you don't have – to enable them to consolidate this position. There are various options:

(a) Slower growth.

(b) Sell some companies and keep others. Unfortunately those with the greatest potential, the ones you will want to invest in if you survive, are just the ones other people want to buy.

(c) Allow the local management and/or staff buy into the company. This should solve the problem of cash, and probably lead to greater gains. After this you will need to look at the proportion of the equity to be sold. Try to keep a controlling interest. Check the company law of the locality: different percentages of shares give minorities rights, and these need to be taken into account.

Conclusion

We could continue on to transfer prices, customs duties and a hundred other items. They all need to be carefully considered, but this book is not the place to do it.

Be suspicious about any foreign investments. As the police sergeant used to say in *Hill St. Blues* – 'Let's be careful out there!' The recent problems of *Ferranti* highlight the wisdom of such advice. The company will probably have to be sold (or a significant part of it), due to fraud found in a U.S. subsidiary. This fraud took place some years earlier –

before it had been bought and become a subsidiary.

A good comercial lawyer is a necessity not a luxury when operating overseas.

CHAPTER TWENTY-TWO

Research and Development – the difference

This is where many U.K. technically-orientated and managed companies go wrong. Your company needs to survive initially, but later to prosper.

In a turnround situation, BASIC RESEARCH, the research into a new area of science in general knowledge terms, should be cut to the bone. In fact, if you are a small company, you should question whether you should be doing it at all. This research is best left to large companies, universities and other public bodies, none of which are usually very cost conscious, but they can, and do, allocate large budgets for it.

Nobel Prize   *Industrial Growth*

Similarly with APPLIED RESEARCH (the application of scientific knowledge in a particular area to see what useful technologies and products can result), ask yourself if some of this work can be hived off to third parties at fixed costs. Make sure that the 'not invented here' scenario isn't taking place.

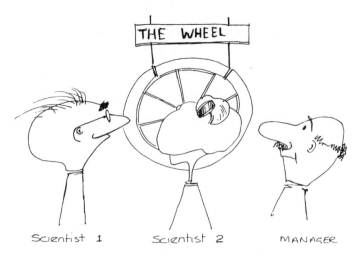

Scientist 1   Scientist 2   MANAGER

1st Scientist	–	*'It will be a great breakthrough'.*
Manager	–	*'Don't XYZ already manufacture a similar range'?*
2nd Scientist	–	*'We are at the leading edge of technology. Where we go, XYZ follows'*
Manager	–	*'But does the market want it? Will they pay extra for it?*
Scientists 1 & 2	–	*'Market? Cost? What have they to do with it'?*

Also, make sure that:

- Each project is to have a budget, not just in currency units, but also in man hours.

- Each project is to have milestones of achievement laid down; the costing and budget is to be compared against these milestones.

- Once a month, a couple of marketing people are thrown in with the research team to brainstorm.

If the budget is 'Y', and you need to stay within this figure, which projects should you continue, start or stop?

Development

This is what the Japanese are good at: teams slowly but

222

surely improving products to give customers the service they want; teams working with improved company performance their goal – not scientific papers and prizes.

Your company needs to think in terms of a wider product market than the specific development you are working on.

In the early 1970s, two engineers and three tradesmen were involved full time in a team working on a development project – a train-like vehicle that could run anywhere in a building, round walls and ceilings, carrying messages, samples, etc. The team never did quite get it to work perfectly; they had to solve technical problem after technical problem, and as a result the train never became a product. Nowadays, we have messages sent via computer post boxes, fax machines and photocopiers in each department (not company as then). So what was the company doing wrong?

(i) It was working on an electro-mechanical device, but ignoring developments in electronics and computing.

(ii) The machine being devised was for the environment of the 1950s and 60s – not the 70s, 80s and 90s.

At the same time, the company was producing simple equipment for offices and shops. If the team's skills had been utilized for improving these products, the company would still be receiving benefits to this day.

General points in the short to medium-term (three months to two years)

(a) Production cost improvements will give benefits first, followed by product improvement if the customer (i) wants it, and (ii) will pay for it. These should take priority over 'pie in the sky' dreams of tomorrow.

(b) Ensure that the teams working on these areas spend only part of their time on development research, and that salesmen (not directors), production workers and marketing are involved with the engineers and scientists.

(c) Ensure that somebody in your organisation or an outside professional, understands Patent Law. This does not mean that you automatically patent everything. In a fast-moving industry, if your competitor is twelve months behind you, you want to keep that advantage.

Licensing fees can be a healthy source of income. If you have the research skills, but not at this time the production, or (more important) marketing and distribution skills and resources, licensing makes economic sense.

Accounting for research and development expenditure

No matter what the arguments for doing so, no part of the development expenditure to date should be capitalised in your financial accounts. This leads to two final points:

1) Why are firms so loath to use others' technology and pay the licencing fees? The fees become a fixed cost to you. You only buy proven technologies. You may not get the Queens Award for Technical Excellence, but you may become – and stay – a highly profitable and healthy company.

2) Most really important developments arise from an engineer tinkering in his garage, somebody who is used to, and needs, a totally unstructured environment.

Become a company always open to new ideas and products. Pay small retainers to such individuals who give you first refusal at *a fair price* for their inventions. It may be that you have someone like this working in your own company. Usually he will make an awful people manager, so don't make him technical director or head of research. Find another title and give him a direct line to the chief executive officer (which at this time is you).

His simple invention changed the world!

Their research did not.

CHAPTER TWENTY-THREE

Selling yourself off for the best price – and a continuing future

Some managers in a turnround situation will be given no choice concerning the eventual sale of the company – the owners will make it for you. In other cases, offers for the company will come out of the blue – people will have been watching your progress. Nothing attracts interest like success.

You now have something that is saleable – *a cash flow*.

Many bodies will come forward with advice and suggestions – there are big fees to be earned. Irrespective of all this advice, you should remember that the company is worth what somebody will pay for it!

What you could value the company on

(a) Discounted value of future cash flows. This is brilliant in theory, but notoriously difficult in practice.

(b) Projected P.E. ratio (price/earnings) compared to market.

(c) The synergy approach. I call this the 2+2 = 5 theory, i.e. fitting your business into another business. The benefits of the combined operations is more than the value to each individual company. An example is the Sky/BSB Satellite TV merger: where the staff of the merged company will constitute 50% less than as two individual companies, their remaining members can now spend their time expanding the market and not fighting over each other.

(d) Management and/or staff buyout. What they are willing to pay to secure their future. They can usually make more of the company than an outsider in a period up to three years.

(e) Strategy approach. Your company is worth a great deal to a large group and you can pick your partner, as demonstrated in the case of Ford/Jaguar: Ford gets a top European quality name which can be sold from its U.S. outlets. For Jaguar it means guaranteed development funds and a degree of independance.

(f) Removal of a competitor. This is similar to synergy but reduces capacity in the market or takes out the aggressive company selling on price.

(g) The opposite of (f) – market entry, for example, buy an EEC company in order to circumvent round trade barriers.

(h) Its assets. This is unlikely if you have turned it round. Perhaps the company could be sold on excess assets plus cash flow.

(i) The management team, but normally members would be approached directly or through head hunters.

What you cannot value a company on

Sentiment! Once you get into a competing bid situation, people just seem to get carried away. Much higher prices can be achieved, not justified by either financial analysis or actual future performance. If the bid is won, the company has massive interest payments to make for the money borrowed to buy the company. This can sink the company, the new owners, or both.

If a bid comes, the owners need to decide if it is acceptable. Are they willing to sell at this price? Any price? Do they wish a negotiated takeover or do they want to get the highest price and thus are willing to encourage other bidders ? There are effects to be taken into account:

Effect on staff

1. Could be positive:

   - 'This guarantees the survival of the company, product, this location, my job'.

2. Could be negative:

   - 'Here we go again'.
   - 'They have an reputation of asset stripping and being ruthless'.
   - 'I thought we were going to continue as a team'.
   - 'My job's at risk again!'

Effect on you

Do you want the company to be sold? Can you do anything about it? Will you? Do you want to stay with the company? Could you work with or for potential acquiring company? Would you put a buyout together and challenge for ownership? Are you by nature and inclination:–

   (a)   an Owner
   (b)   an Entreprenurial Manager
   (c)   a Company Man

If I was committed to a company, the last thing I would want is to lose control of it. Control is not the same as ownership.

CHAPTER TWENTY-FOUR

Strategy
Who are your competitors?

It is amazing how many companies don't know what they are really selling or what their cost base is.

Often they don't know what market(s) they are in. Who is their competition? Who is the potential competition? Where are potential new markets? What are the implications of new technology or for new products?

Nothing I am going to write about here is very new, but I have picked what I believe to be important. The position of this chapter is deliberate. When you are in a crisis situation, you have to concentrate your energies into sorting out today and today's problems and products. Once you have got the company on its feet, you can concentrate on strategy.

Some consultancies do nothing but strategy as do many senior executives. You personally might not be skilled at it. You may use a third party, but it may just as easily be possible to do it in-house.

Just as often the best salesman is an awful sales director, so a good turn roundman can often be a poor strategist.

One of the best strategic thinkers I ever came across was a very poor day to day manager. All poor day to day managers are not good strategic thinkers – they are usually poor at this as well!

SO LET'S START

Marketing

At business school, session after session we had the four P's (or possibly 5). It seemed very simplistic, but I believe it to be very powerful. Product, price, promotion, place (and maybe packaging). Analyse all your products or proposed products to this classification. If you have a product range of 8000, you obviously choose product groups in this case.

<u>Swot Analysis</u>

What are our   –   Strengths

               –   Weaknesses

               –   Opportunities

               –   Threats

Don't do it just once. Repeat it every six months. Do it for the company, the industry, individual products, specific markets. It concentrates the brain on essentials.

Brain Storming

I used to be very sceptical about this. Many people operate their own version. However, I once attended a well run practical evening course on it. Structured, it can be very powerful. What is it doing under strategy? Well, if you want to look at your position you have to fire off some new slants (insights).

Boston Matrix

This I still think a useful tool, especially in a turnround situation. It makes you think, and probably in a form you are not used to. It involves drawing a matrix showing size and growth of markets and positioning your products in it. You will have concentrated up to now on the 'cash cows'. You should have eliminated the 'dogs'. Little if anything will have been done about the 'stars'. You have had neither the time or probably the cash.

An interesting extension of this was explained by Mr McDonald (now professor at the Cranfield Business school). He drew the matrix, then he positioned the products. Then he drew a circle for each product, based on the size of its turnover. This emphasises where your business as a whole is placed. I am sure this has now been further developed. Again, I believe that the real advantage of this technique is to make you think, and probably in a form you are not used to.

Market Share

Studies prove (or so they say) that a dominant market share will lead to high profitability. It is logical – if I have 70% of the market for XYZ's then I should have 70% of promotion funds available and possibly more of the research budget. I should also be the lowest cost producer.

REMEMBER:

a)   First identify the market segment.

There are some powerful possibilities here to get your analysis wrong.

'My product Whisky has 10% of UK spirit market. I have 3% of the UK Whisky market. This market is stagnant and not expected to grow. So, no market share, declining market – milk it'.

Think again. :

'My product is Malt Whisky. The market is growing at 10% per year. All my production is in this segment. I have 25% of the market and my nearest rival has 10%. ' Suddenly the product is a star with a real future.

b) Alternative uses.

You produce pen knives. These can be produced cheaply in many developing countries. You am based in one of the most expensive countries in the world with a small static population. The main growth in pen knife usage is the third world. Main uses in developed world, pencil sharpening and cleaning pipes (both declining). So, low market share. Low cost competitors. Price competition. You are a high cost producer. Your market is declining. GET OUT? WRONG! Product is Swiss Army Knife, manufactured to very high standards. It has numerous useful attachments. Now a compact tool, even a status symbol. Sells for a premium.

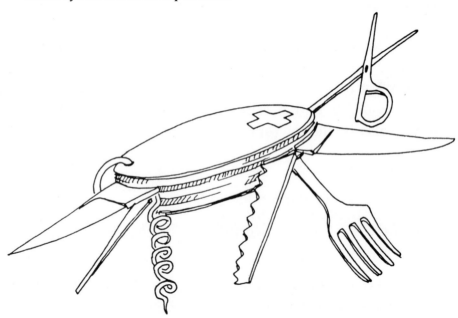

A Swiss 'Star'

c) Fashion.

It is the 1970's. The firm had been in business 100 years. It had only one shop in a small town in a small US State. In addition it operated a mail order business. It was still producing clothing products which had not changed in style for at least 50 years, products made by old labour-intensive methods in the USA. It didn't produce in low cost countries. It had never actively tried to export.

Well, you say, this is a no-hope case; wrong product, wrong country for both sale and production, no distribution. A definite no-hope situation. WAIT A MINUTE, WHAT HAS THIS TO DO WITH FASHION?

The company is J.C. Bean in Maine, USA. They produce outdoor clothing and equipment to the highest standards of ruggedness. Their sales in the US grow and grow. One hundred years of personal recommendation. They even have a growing export market via people requesting cataloges, of just making straight purchase, cash with order. It had become fashionable for executives and others to be seen in this type of clothing in their leisure time. They are 'real men'. In their minds they would have been pioneers in a different age, and they dress the part. The clothing quality is also first class.

Sensitivity Analysis.

You are doing forecasts – what if this happens, or that happens? So you have some figures and some assumptions. Let's say you are going to borrow money. Now, if you cannot repay the principal and interest on it eventually, you will lose the company. So let's increase interest rates to a higher level than you expect and both cut sales and increase your costs, but not your prices. If the model shows that even then you will be able to cover the outgoings, you have a solid proposal.

Forget all the fancy mathematical formulae. This is what sensitivity analysis sets out to answer. If in your model you cannot in the worst situation, cover all your outgoings, at least you will appreciate the level of risk you are taking on.

You can then monitor the actual situation and take appropriate action as necessary.

Probability Analysis

Can be used on its own or very effectively combined with sensitivity analysis. I find that the mathematically orientated, particularly those who are poor with people, love probability. It seems to offer them a detached way of managing by numbers without having to interact with unpredictable and illogical people.

BUT, the probability attached to each item is subjective – you guess it. (call it estimate if you wish). Once you accept that the probability figures you are using are informed guesses, you can really start to gain from the exercise.

What is the reasoning behind the figures you have come up with for the various probabilities? It is very powerful when several people independently assess the probabilities of each item. Then compare the reasoning. Look at the results of your model. Remember they are a guide.

The World, The Environment, The Future

Plenty of people and publications are offering this service. There is also your own trade press. Remember – the trade press you are reading now may not be the trade you are going to be in in the future.

Personally, for an investment of two hours a week, I find the Economist magazine takes some beating. I have certainly worked in some remote spots and have found that by reading this I have kept well up to date.

Competition

OK you say, forget the long term future! Who are they now? If you don't know at least some of them, start the book again – you are going to need it!

You can buy or read market studies. Any decent commercial library will be able to come up with several sources. You can buy international information off data bases. Be careful, most of these studies, if they are in print they are already partially out of date.

For individual company information, Dun & Bradstreet reports or those by CCM, especially on individual addresses in the UK, contain vast amounts of useful information. You can read up directors' backgrounds in various publications. Remember that there might well be a couple of your competitor's salesmen who you really could do with identifying.

Also remember, it is the trends not the absolutes which you are looking for. For instance, total sales of Product X are $XYZ million – very interesting! This is 4% up on last year, our market share is 5% of the total market. The market grew 6% last year. Our market share is up 1% – useful, relative information.

In many industries, it is the product not the firm which is key. Thus competitors are amongst the first purchasers of their competitor's newest car or whatever. They then proceed to take it apart, both physically and by analysing its specifications.

Conclusion

There are many people out there making a good living out of coming up with new techniques – often rehashed old ones which make them a fortune on the lecture circuit.

So now you have examined your competitors and the market and you have your strategy.

> JUST HOW ARE YOU GOING TO PUT IT INTO PRACTICE?
>
> IN WHAT TIME SCALE?
>
> WHO IS GOING TO PUT IT INTO PRACTICE?

It is called analysis paralysis.

Everybody (100%) concentrates on the 'What's'.
>What is the competition?
>What is the future? etc.

Some (75%) concentrate on the 'Where's'.
>Where are we going?
>Where do we want to go?

Less (10%) will be interested in the 'When's'
>When will this happen?
>When will we react?

Virtually none (0.1%) will concentrate on the 'HOW'S'

WITHOUT THE 'HOW'S', STRATEGY IS JUST AN EXPENSIVE FORM OF DAY DREAMING.

CHAPTER TWENTY-FIVE

Crisis Over – Time to leave?

Assuming that you have successfully completed your mission and the company has been turned round, you will almost certainly need a break. Completing a successful turnround operation does have some side effects that need considering!

Having created order from chaos you will probably have developed an affection for both the company and some of its staff. You can hardly expect love in return but you will have earned a considerable degree of respect.

Some people thrive under pressure. Most don't. Those who do will not see it as 'pressure', they will see it as a challenge. If your work has been successful, you will probably be seeking a new challenge. Before now you probably won't have had much time to think about leaving. Perhaps you only took the job on for a specified period. Perhaps other companies who have watched your performance will head hunt you. It may be, if you have been employed by a group, that it has other ideas for you (who knows, a bigger mess to sort out). Alternatively, you may just be fired – 'He's done the job we brought him in for. We don't need him any more.'

Either way, it's time for this company to run under its own management. Is this a job for you? In a fast growing industry, you can probably continue as Chief Executive. In a slow industry, a chairmanship is probably the best position – you can then get involved elsewhere and keep a watchful eye on this operation.

Whatever your decision, you are likely to be in demand – 'You need experience to turn a company round – but you cannot turn a company round without experience.'

NOTHING ATTRACTS LIKE SUCCESS

YES 25% OFF ONE DAYS CONSULTANCY
FROM THE AUTHOR MR. BOFFEY,
TO THE PURCHASERS OF THIS BOOK

NAME

ADDRESS / TEL No

I BOUGHT THIS BOOK FROM

CONDITIONS:-

Only for Asssignments carried out in England, Scotland, Wales.
Discount is off Standard Fee. Full Expenses Incurred Payable.
Only valid for Pages Received by 31st Dec 1993.
Offer only valid for Pages Received not for Photocoples of Pages

SEND TO   DISOS BUSINESS CENTRE
50 SPRINGFIELD ROAD
GATLEY
CHEADLE
CHESHIRE
SK8 4PF